I'm so I
decided to cross
our paths --
With my
warmest wishes -
Cleo

Can You Enjoy Being A Woman?

Can You Enjoy Being A Woman?

A GUIDE TO GETTING WHAT YOU WANT IN A MAN'S WORLD

Cleo Neiman

This book was printed in the United States of America.

To order additional copies of this book, contact:
Xlibris Corporation
1-888-7-XLIBRIS
www.Xlibris.com
Orders@Xlibris.com

Contents

This book is dedicated to my mother
who always came through for me
when I needed her.

AUTHOR'S NOTE

My grown daughters and I represent generations
as diverse as an oil portrait and a Polaroid photo.
When we asked each other the question,
"Do you enjoy being a woman?"—notably, none of us
responded with a resounding
"yes" or *"no."* There was a great deal of hesitation
and a lot of conditional response such as:
*"Well, maybe if . . .", "Sometimes . . .",
"Not always . . ." and "Only when . . ."*
The next question is the one that launched
this book:

"Can you enjoy being a woman?"

* * *

PREFACE

$\mathcal{T}$HE SWING OF the pendulum has finally shattered the myth, like a bull through a cobweb. Women cannot be the same as men.

Crusades against gender imbalance have been raging for so long that the identity of the crusaders has been erased in the name of the *cause*. And the *cause* has blurred over the years as the various leaders of the crusades—with their sexuality camouflaged—dart in and out of their own agendas.

Each of us slides into this world with the same body and instincts that Eve once possessed and that Adam couldn't resist. The very second their eyes met had to be the true beginning of electricity and frankly, little has changed when it comes to creating sparks between men and women.

For instance, looking back in time, we see those ingeniously crafted whalebone corsets of yesteryear, designed to whittle a female's waist and whet a man's appetite. And not to be outdone today—women wear carefully constructed Wonderbras, pushing the breasts up and out, as if to display them on a shelf. Apparently, the feminine need to awaken the masculine need is still very much alive.

Another view in our rear view mirror reveals the land-mark emergence of women's liberation. After simmering for centuries, the seeds of emancipation eventually came to a boil, erupted into an embittered rebellion, then blended into an orchestrated mutiny that threatened the long-sacred privileged stance of men. With pent-up anger—no doubt going back to the first caveman who grabbed a female by the hair and dragged her back to his cave—women lashed out, figuratively castrating men and in some instances, literally.

History has taught us, however, that you don't use a guil-lotine to cure dandruff. When women finally did find a voice, the language was militant. As recently as ten years ago, women were told by the feminist movement that we should rise up and let the world know we are the same as men. We should dress like men, march into the work force, take on male ag-gressors—real and imagined—and fight. The ideal female had to be perfect in every way—at work, at home, in the nurs-ery, in the bedroom. The introduction of the birth control pill unleashed the real meaning of female sexual freedom. Following in its wake, the feminist movement rose to breath-taking heights, soared for a millisecond, then slowly faded into a smoldering hype of hypocrisy—revealing many tight-fisted heroines wearing garter belts beneath their armor.

After spending centuries accepting the dainty and deli-cate identities that men gave them, women were stripped of their frills and expected to act like men. This meant, of course, that men were goaded into acting like women. Who knew where this fanaticism would lead? In our zeal to bring men to their knees, women have lost stature. It is definitely time for females to get elegance and femininity back into their lives.

It is time to acknowledge that women are no longer vic-tims and men are not enemies. Today, women are getting and giving mixed signals—encouraged to act like men but remain women. Women are like teenagers balancing on the high wire between childhood and adulthood. Furthermore, women can't go back and live by the rules their grandmothers followed because inherited standards are not always appropriate to deal with the realities as we know them now. Women can—*and should*—however, pick and choose the pearls of wisdom that have withstood the test of time and string them into the present.

Women are no longer educated for dependency or denied the skills that insure their financial independence. Women now have choices and must ultimately take responsibility for these choices. ***The challenge for a woman is NOT to change human nature or reinvent herself. The challenge for a woman is to bring into harmony her pursuit of independence along with her pursuit of love and companionship.***

* * *

CHAPTER ONE

"SEX AS AN ATTITUDE—NOT AN ACT"

*B*Y TRADITION, *A man's sexual identity is integrated with his ability to accomplish endeavors that women could not or were not allowed to accomplish. Now of course, this tradition has been challenged and sexual expectations of both men and women have changed dramatically—as if a long-running show has been re-written and re-cast.*

Steps between lovers now falter because of the uncertainty of their roles. Who should take the lead? If she is aggressive, should he retreat? If his performance is uneven, should she demand more rehearsal or find a new partner? Furthermore, standing ovations don't always mean success.

* * *

Why can't sex be as simple for humans as it is for animals?

Life obviously would be a lot easier if humans mated just once a year like penguins do. However, mention that concept to men and you'll find out why they hate to wear tuxedos.

The human female, unlike the female animal, can have sexual relations pretty much any time she chooses. The human female doesn't have to wait until her biological "season" comes around.

The human male sex drive, on the other hand, is very much like the animal male sex drive: simple and straight forward. If the female's available—he's available! However, the male animal, unlike the male human, is kept in line by the *biological* readiness of the female animal. The human male, of course, is kept in line instead by the *emotional* readiness of the human female—which, admittedly can be a challenge, but nevertheless, most often surmountable.

The unrelenting sexual urgency of the human male can also be complicated by demands put upon him by family as well as society in general. These *interferences* can obviously affect sexual performance, which is why a man will take a mistress as well as a wife, so that he can satisfy his basic sexual desires and still justify the moral demands that society places on family.

Is the human sex drive as all consuming as it appears to be?

There are actually <u>three</u> certainties in life: death, taxes and sex.

Sexual expression is very much a part of life. The sex drive exists from the moment of birth until the last breath is taken. It is a dynamic, compelling force in our lives and affects literally everything we do—the way we dress, what we dream, how we think, what we say, and how we act.

The nature and expression of sexual urges varies, of course, with each individual, but the sex drive—installed securely in the brain—is always in gear, even in someone who may *appear* to be asexual. For instance, the sex drive can be "re-routed" or re-focused into protracted working hours (that workaholic you know may just be working out his sexual frustrations); or sexual energy can be channeled into other activities such as athletics. Temporary "detours" can also occur in one's sex drive, depending upon events in life, like separation or divorce.

What is the one primary difference between a man's and woman's basic sexual instinct?

A man wants to conquer and a woman wants to be conquered. And that's only the tip of the iceberg! Beneath the surface of this simple difference is the complicated mechanism that either floats the boat or sinks the ship.

Wanting to conquer or to be conquered are unconscious desires, or basic instincts, that most people have. However—unlike the animal kingdom—the desires or instincts of human beings are tempered by societal and environmental influences: i.e., what your parents taught you, what society dictates as the "appropriate" feminine or masculine roles of the times, etc. In our current culture, the perception of men as sole providers and power figures is pretty much a memory from bygone eras. However, the *male instinct* remains and every man's secret desire to fulfill this role is still very much alive.

Consider the story of Annette and Robert as a classic example of the dynamics involved in a man's and woman's basic sexual instincts: Annette and Robert had a successful relationship that was headed for marriage when fate intervened in the form of family pressures. Wedding plans were canceled and shortly thereafter, Annette and Robert separated. Subsequently, each married other mates and the years flowed together as their lives took separate paths.

After eight years, Annette's marriage failed and she filed for divorce. Time had nibbled away the bitterness of her breakup with Robert and she found herself now savoring some of the sweet memories of their relationship. When she heard from a mutual friend that he had moved out of town she started to wonder what he was doing and if he was happy.

After much soul searching, Annette decided to track down his phone number. It sat on her desk for weeks. One evening she found the courage and made the call.

To her delight and amazement, she learned that Robert had just recently been divorced also. He said he had been thinking about her, too and wanted desperately to see her. After juggling various schedules, they arranged for Annette to travel to where Robert was now living. He urged her to stay at least a week, but she insisted she could only stay four days.

As Annette made arrangements for the trip, her emotions seesawed from exhilaration to fear. She and Robert had not discussed on the phone where she would stay, but she knew that Robert intended for her to stay with him. Annette had to admit that she would love to run to Robert's bed, but her instincts were waving red flags, so Annette decided that she would stay in a hotel—by herself.

Why? *Because men like to conquer.* If she ran to his bed right away, where's the challenge for him? By moving cautiously and allowing time to get reacquainted, the relationship is not only being renewed on a stronger foundation, but more importantly, Robert has the opportunity to pursue Annette and eventually win her over. This is, of course, the ultimate victory for a man and a tremendous boost to his masculine ego.

Annette did stay in a hotel and Robert did protest. However, Annette did not back down; therefore, Robert increased his efforts to court her. In the end, Robert happily became the conquering hero and Annette happily became his bride.

Men do like to pursue an elusive woman—the fun is in the chase. A woman may protest loudly to the world that she is tough and independent, but instinctively, she would like to be protected by a man. A woman, also—underneath all of her bravado—longs to "save" the man she loves. Consider the ongoing popularity of the movie, "Casablanca" as a good example of the classic desire of a female to use her powers of femininity to transform a man from a cruel, heartless cad into a caring, responsible human being.

Understanding sexual instincts is easy when it comes to animals—but coping with it in humans is pretty much like trying to nail Jello on the wall.

How are men's and women's sex drives different?

If you believe the theory that blood can rush to only one spot at a time, you'll find that when it comes to sex drive, a man's blood rushes south, whereas a woman's blood turns north to the brain.

When a man isn't thinking about sex, itself, he's probably thinking about what he can do to get *more* of it. With women, it's not that straightforward; when women think about sex, it's tied to emotional factors or other outside influences. Men are more matter-of-fact; women are more romantic.

A man's sexual urges are compelling and primarily driven by biological and hormonal factors. A woman's sex drive is more complicated—driven to some extent by hormones—but predominately by the complexities of emotion. Ideally, before a woman can connect sexually with a man, she needs to build an emotional bridge that will support her responses. Women have the ability to enjoy a wider range of sexual experiences—from cuddling to intercourse—and feel satisfied.

A man's sex drive is more insulated against "outside" distractions than a woman's. For instance, the color of the

draperies or the wrong choice of music can turn a woman off.
Whereas in the same setting, the man won't even be aware
that there *ARE* draperies or music!

Does this difference in sex drive give women more power?

Count on it. It's called demand looking for supply.

For centuries, men have risked empires, careers and
family for the sake of sex—a startling fact when you realize
that a man might put his entire future in peril for an act that
could be measured in a matter of minutes.

Is there anything wrong with a woman using sex to get something she wants?

Not at all. If the promise of sex can be used to your advantage, you'd be foolish to deny yourself that edge.

Waving the 'carrot' of sexual satisfaction in front of a
man is a terrific incentive. Advertising agencies have been
using this method for years to sell everything from after-shave
to condoms. Besides, turnabout is certainly fair play. Men are
experts at waving 'carrots' in front of women—promising
them everything from dinner to diamonds if they'll have sex
with them.

Bartering for sex has been around since time began; it's
an extremely successful *tool* when used wisely—you can even
"price gouge" if the moment is right.

Do some men still feel that they have to "possess" the woman?

There's something about choosing a woman you like, grab-
bing her by the hair and dragging her to your cave that makes
a man feel like he's really in charge. Men always have and
always will feel the need to conquer and supposedly, when
you conquer something in the literal sense, it's yours!

However, in our modern-day, sophisticated, equal rights, affirmative action, feminist and anti-chauvinistic world, men have to settle for drinks and dinner and lots of begging. Of course, "domesticating" the human male doesn't necessarily alter his fantasy life. In fact, it might encourage it. What man doesn't get a testosterone rush when he fantasizes about making a woman his "toy?"

Are there women who object to the male dominant position in the sexual act?

Yes, there are a surprising number of women who do. Their hostility toward men is carried into the bedroom where resentment of a man's *natural* aggressiveness is demonstrated by acting cold and unresponsive. Of course, hostility of this nature would obviously be manifested in other areas of a relationship, such as arguments over money decisions, social commitments, career choices, etc.

Are men as sexually confident as they act?

Almost never. An overt display of sexual confidence is usually an act of bravado very much like whistling in the dark.

Most men don't really know *what* they're doing or *how* they're doing it. They just know they *have* to do it and hope it comes out right. Age plays a major role in a man's sexual confidence, as he eventually learns that what he's doing in bed involves another human being.

Of course, the more sexually "knowledgeable" a woman is, the more insecure a man might feel. When a woman doesn't really understand who she is or what she wants, a man can pretty much get away with doing whatever he wants sexually. But when a woman knows who she is and exactly what she wants, expectations are much higher.

What should a woman do when a man can't perform?

Tread softly. A woman is in an almost frightening position of power because a man is *extremely* vulnerable when this happens.

Establishing and maintaining an erection is a mysterious and mystical process for most men and if the process fails them, they are totally devastated.

Telling the man that you "don't mind" is frankly pointless. A man's main concern at this time is rooted in something far more primitive and fundamental than the need to satisfy his partner. When a man cannot perform, he is literally *afraid*.

The best way for a woman to react in this situation is to appear confident—reassuring the man that this is something temporary and that variations in performance are certainly normal. And, of course, they are.

Men instinctively equate sexual potency with strength. If a man's performance falters, the reaction of his partner is crucial to his continuing confidence and self esteem. Intimacy isn't about always being available; the key to intimacy is trust and comfort.

Can a woman build up a man's sexual confidence?

Yes, by realizing that every man has an Achille's heel: his masculinity—the one area where he is most vulnerable.

Behind all the bravado, the boasting and the chest beating, most men have nagging doubts about size, competence and endurance—especially as a man moves further from the days of youthful stamina. A woman who understands these instincts and fears can reach behind the macho facade and provide the needed support to keep his masculinity strong and intact. For instance, a woman can let a man know she thinks he's a great lover, that she admires him and especially important, she should let him know she needs him. Of course, this support has its own rewards for the woman, too: a heightened sense of *mutual* satisfaction.

Is there a sure-fire way that a woman can satisfy a man sexually?

Obviously, every man (as well as every woman) has his own "unique" sexual fantasies as well as individual likes and dislikes. However there is one approach for a woman that almost always guarantees a sexually satisfied man: when a woman is confident and content with her own self image, she is able to *go beyond her own needs* to understand the man's emotional *as well as* his physical requirements.

It's important to remember that the sexual act is an act of *sharing*—not showing.

Do you have to have a good face and body to be sexually appealing?

Contrary to what the advertisements tell us, sex appeal doesn't come from high heels, short skirts and eye shadow. That's transient mating at best. Furthermore, sex appeal doesn't suddenly appear after you've liposuctioned the fat from your thighs and recycled it to your butt. You can't buy sex appeal— it is one of the few things in life that's free.

True sex appeal is warmth, a show of openess and a spontaneous love of life. It has long been a fact of life that "plain" women know more about men than beautiful women do. That's because a woman who knows about men gains confidence. Sex appeal is definitely the fire that is ignited by a woman's confidence.

How does a woman create sexual desire?

It's not the steak, it's the *sizzle*. More precisely, it's suggestibility—like whispering in a man's ear that you're double-jointed and watching his eyes glaze over.

Imagination is always far more intriguing that reality. For instance, a "subtle" bathing suit that covers the essentials, leaving just enough to create some interest, is far more appealing that a skimpy bathing suit consisting of three decals and a string.

When a woman is happy with the way she looks and is comfortable with her body, *that* is what should show and that's very appealing to a man. But there's another important factor: A beautiful body may look interesting to a man, but what also captures his attention is a shy smile that suggests frailty. Men find any kind of *vulnerability* totally irresistible.

A smart woman—one who truly enjoys being a woman—will *always* find some way to make a man feel needed. She may be extremely accomplished in her own right, but she'll be clever enough to allow some frailty to show through.

Do women have as many sexual fantasies as men do?

Yes, however female sexual fantasies are not nearly as well *publicized* as male fantasies. Women are not as willing to verbalize their fantasies and in some cases, will try to suppress them out of fear or embarrassment.

The seeds of sexual fantasy take root in the unconscious during childhood and continue to develop and evolve throughout a person's lifetime. Allowing oneself to explore "secret" fantasies is a very productive way to build self esteem. Drawing upon sexual fantasies is a healthy way for a woman to improve sexual performance by freeing inhibitions and thereby reducing anxiety.

What is an aphrodisiac for men?

Probably the best is pornography. Sexy magazines and videos—not porn with violence—can be a healthy stimulus.

Younger men are stimulated visually, while older men

need both visual and physical stimulation. Pornography is a good supplementary outlet for a man, plus it can be an educational tool for those who are less experienced and want to improve technique.

Pornography allows a man to deal openly with his desires and it allows couples to explore fantasies together, thereby enhancing erotic pleasure for both.

Is size really important in sex?

Only is fantasy—not in reality.

The dimension of a woman's breasts, for example, is certainly not as important as the dimension of her focus on her partner.

With a man, it's definitely not the size of the ship that counts, it's his ability to stay in port until all the passengers have disembarked.

Should a woman talk dirty with her lover?

Why not—unless the lover objects? Erotic talk can definitely add another dimension to lovemaking. Talking is communication and the more communication, the better in *all* interpersonal relationships.

How should a mate react when a man is obsessed with sex?

A lot depends on the "degree" of obsession. A true sexual compulsion is a serious behavioral problem that usually indicates a deep self-destructive tendency.

A man who is "constantly preoccupied" with sex is usually very insecure in his manhood—an insecurity that most often has its roots in some childhood trauma. As an adult, therefore, he will require constant reinforcement to prove to himself that he is powerful.

A man obsessed with sex is pretty much like a vacuum cleaner with insomnia. Trade him in for a new model with a better on and off switch.

Can sexual promiscuity be considered an illness?

There are endless jokes about sexual promiscuity—such as "the woman who has seen more pricks than a dart board." However, there are varying definitions of this uncontrolled behavior.

Sexual promiscuity of short duration can often be attributed to reactive causes such as a dissolved love affair, divorce, etc. In cases like this—through excess—one usually learns moderation.

Long-term sexual abandon, on the other hand, has very different and more serious connotations. In this case, the promiscuous person often has a severe lack of identity and/or has an overwhelming fear of becoming attached to any one person.

Violence against women is often sexualized in the movies. Why isn't violence against men sexualized?

Because it doesn't sell tickets.

Erotic violence against women is a sure draw for a large male audience. Movie makers understand all to well the primitive male fantasy to dominate and degrade the female.

Domesticated and sophisticated "modern men," of course, will verbalize protests against sexual violence, however, they will still be first in line when it comes to experiencing it vicariously. The idea of sexual domination definitely triggers a man's instincts in the most *primal* way.

Why are women so often accused of being castrating females?

Of course, this is a figurative or symbolic statement. With *rare* exceptions, men are not *literally* afraid that women will castrate them since men are usually physically stronger than most women.

Basically, men just hate to be threatened—especially by a woman. The castration fears that men express are related to childhood experiences and relationships with a mother, aunt, grandmother, etc.

One way to understand castration anxiety is to look at the *unconscious* symbolism of sexual intercourse whereby a man allows a woman to *take* his most prized possession and once he has surrendered his strength to her, he is weak and *powerless.*

Sigmund Freud—the author of "penis envy"—proposed the theory that women were jealous of men because they didn't have that "floppy accessory." Men, of course, believe strongly in this theory.

Women, on the other hand, are generally amused by the theory and frankly mystified: "Why would any woman want that droopy thing flopping around between their legs—especially when it doesn't even come with a guarantee? Sometimes it functions and sometimes it doesn't!"

Why does a man act passionate sometimes and indifferent at other times?

You can usually trace this ambivalence back to the 'triangulation' crisis of his adolescent years when his budding sexual feelings, his love for his mother, plus society's demands for him to be tough all collide in a love-hate tug of war.

Translation: A man will be warm and fuzzy in an effort to win you. Then, when he feels he's getting too close to you—or worried that he's getting too soft and losing his male identity—he'll back off and appear distant. After a while, he'll return once more to win you over. Obviously, a woman should not take this behavior *personally* since it stems from a man's long-standing fear of dependency and attachment.

Most men are plagued with the never-ending predicament of not wanting to get too close, *yet* not wanting to get too far away. Of course, this presents difficulties in intimate relationships. However, if the woman understands the origin of the difficulties, the resolution of any problems is a lot easier.

When a man complains that he "can't win" an argument with a woman, what he's really saying is, "If I give in to her and lose the argument, then she's reeled me in too close; if I fight to win the argument, I'll still be losing because I'll be kept at a distance."

Confronting a man directly about his indifference can often cause more anxiety and apprehension, since he will feel the need to defend himself. He probably won't even realize that he has been distant and the confrontation will only cause him to retreat further.

In most cases, the best way to handle this situation is to allow a man time and space to *regroup* his masculine resources. Once he regains his confidence, he'll be back warm and fuzzy all over again.

What does it mean when a man's sexual interest fades over an extended period of time?

Usually, when this happens, a woman will blame herself— like maybe she's gained too much weight, or maybe there's another woman.

If both of these possibilities are unlikely, the answer to the problem might just lie with the man, himself. The way people relate sexually depends upon how they relate to themselves. If a man is feeling inadequate because of his work or some other problem he is personally experiencing, he will feel inadequate sexually.

The best medicine for this malaise is *feminine* support. He doesn't need a mother and he doesn't need a friend; he needs a female to reassure him that in her eyes, he can hang the moon.

Should a woman be mysterious to maintain a man's interest?

Most definitely! A woman without mystery is like an egg without salt.

Some women righteously announce to the world that they will never keep anything from their husbands—failing to realize that there's a huge difference between lying and not revealing everything. Some things are better left unsaid, like confessing every last detail of a previous ill-fated romance. Basically, women who tell all, feel insecure and seek approval and relief from some self-imposed guilt—rationalizing that they are doing so because they have no secrets.

Alfred Hitchcock once said that *"Women should be like a good suspense movie. The more left to the imagination, the more excitement there is."*

Is there a danger is having sex too early in a relationship?

Very definitely, because relationships should advance in levels, like climbing a staircase.

The story of Rachel and Allen is a good example of the risks involved in skipping steps: When Rachel and Allen first met, it appeared to be a happy accident of fate. They were both reaching for the same book in the biography section of the book store. Before long, they were sitting over coffee talking about their mutual interest in biographies and comparing notes on the books they had read. They made a date for dinner the next evening.

Allen appeared to be an easy-going man with a great deal of charm. Rachel felt relaxed as she sat across the table from him, listening attentively as he broke off small pieces of his life for her. She told herself she was liking what she heard. Following dinner, they took advantage of the beautiful summer evening and walked several blocks to a nearby lounge to listen to some jazz—another thing they had in common.

One hour chased the next and before they knew it, the musicians were packing up and everyone was leaving. Allen suggested she stop by his place for coffee. He boasted that he made the meanest cup of cappuccino in town.

Rachel hesitated, knowing that saying 'yes' to coffee meant agreeing to spend the night. She also knew that saying 'no' would be the wisest thing to do. Reluctantly, she declined. He insisted. She gave in.

It was, by all measure, a lovely night. So was the next night and the night after that. Rachel allowed her fantasies to flower. Why not—she told herself. Allen seemed to be the 'perfect' man.

Two weeks later, Allen called to break a date, saying he had to take care of something for his mother. Rachel felt hurt but rationalized that he was just being a good son. More broken dates followed and Rachel's rationalizations grew thin. When she finally confronted Allen, he got defensive. The evening ended in a heated argument, with Rachel leaving in anger.

As she came to realize later, the anger she felt was directed mostly at herself. If only, she had gotten to know Allen first before making an emotional investment, she wouldn't be feeling such a loss.

When all of the truths finally surfaced, Rachael discovered that in fact, Allen's mother had died when he was a child. Furthermore, he was breaking dates with Rachel to go out with another woman he had been dating for over a year.

Does having sex with a man mean you're in a committed relationship with him?

Only if you *both* agree.

Up until recently, women were pretty much bound by rigid tradition when it came to sex—"Don't have it until you're married." If a woman did have sex with a man before marriage, in most cases, commitment was definitely on her mind, if not his.

But as the popular saying goes . . . "You've come a long way, baby." Today, women are entering into sexual relationships in the same fashion as men do. Of course, a lot of men who would ideally like women to behave in a"traditional" manner find women's sexual emancipation troubling. Men have enjoyed a very privileged position in the past and it's difficult for them to give that up.

In any event, one truth remains: relationships are like seesaws. And since two ends of a seesaw cannot be elevated at the same time, the best way for two people to establish balance is to make sure that one doesn't climb aboard without the other one intending to do the same.

Does passionate sex always mean love?

Not necessarily. Men have certainly been able to enjoy *good* sex without being in love. Now women have finally earned that freedom.

A no-strings attached sexual liaison can be very rewarding depending upon the time and place in your life. Since sexual relations uncluttered by love usually serve to intensify emotional isolation, it is often *more* of a challenge for women to enjoy strictly sexual interludes than for men. However, it certainly can be done.

For instance, Katy, a woman in her early 20's, decided

she wanted to pursue her profession and not make any kind of long term commitment until at least her mid-30's. Of course, this meant that Katy had to make a very strong conscious effort to restrict her own emotional involvement. Katy told each "new lover" from the start that he had no rights whatsoever over her and furthermore, if he was smart, he wouldn't claim any. Some stayed and some left, but Katy remained true to her pledge.

Passion can be a powerful and therapeutic analgesic; it should be welcomed in whatever doses are available. Very little else in this world can offer such magic.

Does a woman's attitude about herself influence her sexual performance?

Most definitely. How a woman feels about herself as a person and how she views her body relate directly to how she performs in bed. Above all, a woman who is confident is more open, less inhibited and much more willing to share.

Another important factor that influences a woman's performance is her expectation of the sexual experience. Unfortunately, most movies and romance novels are misleading, offering more fancy than fact. In true life, timing is not consistently perfect; two people don't always shriek out in unison, like two opera singers reaching high notes simultaneously. Also, in the real world of erotic adventures, hair does get mussed up, mascara will get smeared and most underwear doesn't "rip" off that easily.

When it comes to sexual experiences, there's no such thing as *average* or *normal*. The type of person you are pretty much dictates the kind of lover you are.

Why does a man admit to a woman that she intimidates him?

Because she probably does. Furthermore, this is not an admission that a man makes easily.

Frequently, a man's sexual attraction to a woman can be so strong, he fears that if he surrenders himself to her, he will be consumed by his need for her and thus be rendered powerless. This fear can literally cause a man to become impotent in his initial sexual attempts.

If a woman is interested in a man who is intimidated by her, what should she do?

Take an airbrush to her responses. A woman doesn't have to "change" herself—she just has to choose carefully which dimension of herself she exposes at first. For instance, when a woman feels a man is intimidated by her, she should try to appear *less threatening* by allowing her soft side to show whenever possible. The more masculine and self assured she makes him feel, the faster his fears will dissipate.

With gentle persuasion and patience a woman can build up a man's ego until he feels that he's in control again. Once this happens, the results are definitely worth the wait.

Can a woman ever change a man?

Only in the movies.

You cannot change someone like changing a shirt. Human beings can only evolve. A man or a woman will only get *more like themselves* as they get older. To think otherwise can only lead to disaster.

Women are especially guilty of romanticizing: seeing what they want to see instead of looking at what a man *really* is and listening to what they want to hear instead of hearing what he's *really* saying.

Does a man's sexual interest change after marriage?

Sometimes boredom is blamed for a man's or woman's waning sexual interest and the obvious answer for this is variety. Sex is like linen—the more you change it, the sweeter.

There's another reason why a man's sexual interest might change after marriage: a change in lifestyle. Keeping in mind that a man's sexual drive is straightforward and basically uncomplicated, the introduction of mental stress or emotional hurdles will often affect his sexual performance.

As an illustration, picture a man who's primary function in life is to go out hunting for food during the day and returning home at night to have sex. Obviously, this man is going to be a better lover than a man who fights for survival in the corporate jungle twelve hours a day, then comes home at night to a schedule of soccer practice, helping with dinner and a neighborhood crime-watch meeting.

It's easy to see why vacations are often viewed as sexual holidays—especially when the man doesn't even have to hunt for food.

Is there anything wrong with having a sexual relationship with a married man?

This is a situation that truly has no right or wrong as long as the man and woman involved *equally* take responsibility for their actions—in particular, take responsibility for the risk of hurting anybody else involved in their lives. If nobody is "holding a gun to anybody's head," people pretty much do what they *want* to do. Any judgment call on a sexual relationship with someone who is married depends totally on the circumstances that surround the relationship.

For instance, a woman might accept the advances of a married man who makes himself available because she doesn't want a commitment. If she's going through a difficult time in her life—like trying to get over a broken heart—this type of relationship might help her get through it. Why the married man is making himself available is his concern and most definitely, *his* responsibility.

Other times—because of emotional or financial responsibilities—a man may be *locked* into a marriage with a wife who has detached herself because of physical limitations or mental deficits.

In some religions, it's actually 'kosher' and encouraged for the husband to have a concubine. It can be a win-win-win situation. The wife is happy because she's not interested in having sexual relations with her husband anymore, plus she has another woman in the house to help with the children. The husband is pleased because his needs are satisfied and the concubine is delighted because she is well taken care of.

Who's to judge?

Do sexual relations change as people get older?

Yes. As a generalization, sex becomes less biological and more an expression of love and sharing.

Women feel more self assured of their bodies and more secure with their sexual performance.

Men, on the other hand become less secure with their sexual performance and more reliant upon the interpersonal bond with their partners.

Are older women better lovers?

Almost always.

One advantage for older women is that they are no longer bound by the fear of conception and can give themselves freely in their sexual relations. As a woman gets older, she has pretty well figured out what she wants; therefore, as her comfort level rises, so does her sex drive.

Also, the more secure a woman becomes with her own sexuality, the more she's able to give to her partner—promising greater benefits for both.

Are older men better lovers?

Usually. When women fake orgasm, it's often because men fake foreplay. That changes as a man gets older.

Younger men are prisoners of their boyish urgencies and self centeredness. When it comes to sex, younger men really don't know *what* they're doing .. they can just do it all night!

Older men, on the other hand, cannot do it all night, but they know what they're doing and spend a lot more time doing it! Older men, eventually become the candlelight and soft music kind of lovers. Even though years may steal fire from the body, the best sex ignites in the mind.

What is the best way to make a mature man feel sexually secure?

Make him feel safe and confident in his masculinity. As his sexual potency wanes, a man needs to be reassured that he is still powerful in other ways and admired for *all* of his strengths. Intimacy and trust become increasingly important to a man as he gets older.

What is the best way to make a mature woman feel sexually secure?

A mature woman doesn't need to feel *sexually* secure. As a woman ages, she doesn't lose sexual potency; if anything she gains some. As her appearance changes, a mature woman needs to be reassured that she still is desirable and still loved.

What is the greatest gift a man can give to a woman?

To listen to her. And the reason this is a 'gift' is that *listening* doesn't come easily to a man. He's got to want to make that effort.

When a man truly pays attention to what a woman feels and what she wants, his devotion is like a magnet. She'll follow him to the ends of the earth.

What is the greatest gift a woman can give to a man?

To encourage him to live up to his expectations of himself.

A man's sexual drive at any age is such an integral part of his sense of self that if his faith in his own masculinity falters, *every other aspect of his life falters.*

By any measure, a package this fragile should be labeled, "Handle with Care."

CHAPTER TWO

"VIVE LA DIFFERENCE—

OR DAMN THE DIFFERENCE"

*T*HE DIFFERENCES BETWEEN *men and women have puzzled philosophers since time began and will inspire lyricists till time runs out. As men and women attempt to cultivate a mutually satisfying existence, it is important to acknowledge and respect the differences inherent in the sexes and not deny their existence by minimizing the vulnerabilities.*

In the past, gender differences for women were viewed in terms of limitations. Now we must examine these differences in terms of possibilities and potentials.

* * *

Why is there so much confusion about gender identity?

One of the underlying reasons is a shift in ideology. For so many years, women were considered weak and their differences from men were looked upon as inferior. With the dawning of feminism, however, suddenly women were pointing the finger at men, labeling *them* weak and inferior.

Today, women don't know *what* they want and men don't know *how* to want. Men complain that women expect too much from them and women complain that men aren't sensitive and don't reveal their thoughts. Men accuse women of not being feminine and women accuse men of being wimps and weaklings.

Instead of acting like surly dogs at the end of a chain, ready to leap at the first misstep, it might be a good idea to pull in the fangs and take a good, hard look at what's right under our noses. The basic instincts of men and women have remained the same since the beginning of time—whether they were dressed in armor or petticoats and corsets, or mini-skirts or leisure suits: *Women looked upon men as heroes and men looked upon women as needing heroes.*

In the past, of course, for the very important reason of financial security, most women *needed* to think of men as heroes—a good match of instinct and reality. Now, however, women are discovering that it's within their power to be their *own heroines*, and with this discovery, men seem to lose their luster. "Who needs men?" a woman will say, but the truth of the matter is that even though a woman may find she can be her own heroine—when it comes to a relationship with a man—she will still *INSTINCTIVELY* want him to be her hero and, of course, he will *INSTINCTIVELY* want to oblige.

The resolution of this dilemma is quite simple: A woman can still feel the independence of being able to take care of herself . . . but, if she's smart, she'll provide enough opportunity for a man to still be her hero—not only in his eyes, but more importantly, in hers.

Why has it taken so long for men to accept women's contributions to society outside the home?

It takes a long time to overcome fear.

Men have always been afraid that if a woman is emancipated, she will cease to exist only for the man. For literally thousands of years, men have dictated that bearing children and maintaining the home was *all* that should be required of a woman.

Men have never been eager to give up this patriarchal stance and women have been forced to accept their limitations either by the pressures of long-standing tradition or the demands of their circumstances. When women did stray from these boundaries, they were made to feel guilty and to this day, some women *still* have feelings of guilt for stepping outside the mold of the time-honored female stereotype.

Those men who resent women who fly in the face of male dominance by leaving the nest, will place undue pressures and stresses on them. And, strangely enough, some of the more vocal critics who promote this guilt are *other women* who are frightened to leave the "confines" themselves and therefore, admonish those women who do.

A frightening example of this occurred recently when a married couple—both professionals with careers outside the home—left their new baby with a sitter during the work week. Tragically, the child died, allegedly abused by the sitter, and the anguished mother—incredible as it may seem—began receiving hate mail from women who berated her for furthering her career instead of staying home with her child.

What are the most common social differences between men and women?

There are many and despite all of the efforts over the years to banish them, the differences between male and female appear very early in life and remain strong till the end.

Men are valued for what they do, women are valued for how they look. Men have definitely built this world, but women have civilized and enlightened it. Women are defensive. Men like to take the offensive; it is men who start wars . For instance, it's pretty obvious that missiles would be shaped differently if women designed them.

Society encourages men to be self sufficient and independent. Women, on the other hand, are encouraged to join relationships. Women apologize even though they have done nothing, men avoid blame even when it's deserved. (For instance, the first time Adam had the chance, he laid the blame on a woman.)

Women will attempt to deal with a sensitive situation, whereas men are far more likely to run from a sensitive situation. If a man is trapped in an uncomfortable setting, he will search for some way to escape, if not physically, then mentally. A classic example of this is the delivery suite at a hospital where the husband's attention is glued to a sports event on TV, while his wife is in labor in a bed right beside him in the same room.

Men and women will tend to cluster in their own gender groups at large parties—not necessarily out of choice. Usually, when a lone woman wanders over to a group of men, her entrance into their circle will signal a change in their conversation and then, slowly but surely, a steady dissolving of the members of the group. A lone man will rarely wander over to a group of women unless he is drunk and/or eager to show off.

Sense of humor is another area of difference: a man's humor is aggressive, physical and sophomoric. A woman's humor tends to be more self critical and passive. In a relationship, women will always feel like they're giving more to make it work—and usually, they are.

Men are genetically and sociologically out to conquer— not compromise. Even in the most sophisticated and advanced societies in today's world, the male is rewarded for being tough and aggressive and the female is rewarded for being compliant and submissive. Basically, man wants to annihilate and woman wants to neutralize.

Sexually, men are high pressure, women are slow flowering. Men spend most of their lives originating, while women spend most of their lives *waiting*.

Women are traditionally very insecure and self-conscious about their bodies and their looks in general. Men, on the other hand, consider themselves to be irresistible no matter what—even though from a woman's perspective, they're about as appealing as a butcher's pencil.

What are some of the mental differences between men and women?

As research has shown, women are characteristically open and giving, while men are more closed. Men tend to take a surgical approach to life, whereas women tend to take more of a medical approach.

Women are better at understanding others than men are. That's why mothers are considered "more important" than fathers when it comes to the emotional support of a child.

Men are less sensitive to pain than women are; however, women appear to be able to cope with pain much better than men since women are able to verbalize their emotions and thereby get support from others.

Studies have shown that women tend to experience more psychological problems such as depression and anorexia than men do. This difference could be explained by cultural and social factors, or by recent findings that reveal women tend to produce less serotonin—a brain chemical that governs mood.

Women are far more multi-dimensional in their moods than men. The macho male ego doesn't allow such things. Hormonal shifts, notwithstanding, one of the joys of being a woman is that she can be multi-dimensional depending upon her desire: athletic, competitive, neutral, warm, frilly, feminine or sexy—it's entirely up to her.

Women, of course, lead with their emotions, whereas men try to disguise theirs. A woman's alcohol intake should definitely be monitored when she is in a highly emotional state, since combining elevated emotions with too many glasses of wine is like releasing the flood gates—once the water has gushed out, it's too late to take it back. What women really need is an "alcohol meter" that can be attached to the phone. If a woman has had "one too many," the minute she opens her mouth, the dial tone would cut off.

Women traditionally have much better memories than men do—which is probably why the sports instant replay was invented.

If men and women are so different, how can a woman ever get a man to 'fully' understand her?

It's difficult at best. Even if you have the world's greatest husband, lover and friend all rolled into one, you can't expect him to read between your lines.

Instead of getting angry or frustrated at his lack of perception, it's far more expedient and far more rewarding to just accept a man's limitations, then go where you'll get the connection and confidence you need—a girlfriend, your mother, your sister, or maybe a women's group.

When you want to explore emotions, don't ask a man to walk in your shoes. Another woman is the only one who can do that comfortably.

Do men complain that women don't understand them?

Hardly. Men know that they are basically simple creatures and that figuring them out is about as easy as peeling the skin off a banana. Men have never claimed to be complex. They have two basic needs: food and sex—or sex and food—depending upon what time of the day it is, or how long it's been since the last meal.

Men are truly fascinating creatures, but the simpleness of their natures can make relationships with women complicated because women are so complex and multi-sided that they too often make the mistake of expecting the *same* out of a man— which is about as absurd as expecting a rooster to lay eggs.

Furthermore, a man doesn't really care about being *understood;* he would rather be trusted and believed in.

Is it possible at all to defy physiology?

History, as well as common sense, has proven it's a waste of time—like putting a rope through the eye of a needle! In our eagerness to be like men, women have tried to make men more like women. *Neither* is going to happen!

Consider some examples of a woman's *fundamental need* to be feminine—even in the most stringent and extreme circumstances:

During World War II, in the 1940's, when stockings were almost non-existent, woman would cover their legs with cocoa or cooking sauces and since cosmetics were in short supply, they used charcoal for eye shadow.

In Sarajevo, women fighting along side the men in trenches would be found wearing lipstick and high-heeled boots along with their fatigues.

And in Beirut, it was common for women to curl their hair and give each other manicures with people fighting on the streets outside their homes.

Today, women in Muslim societies—who are prohibited by law to show any part of their bodies—wear sexy lingerie and designer clothes beneath their black chadors.

Instead of trying to defy physiology, our energies would

be better spent fighting for equality—*not because we think we're the same as men*—but because every human being should have the equal right to accept his own differences and have those differences accepted by others.

Are women genetically superior to men?

By all accounts, yes. Women live longer and bear more physical pain than men. Also, look at the *tools* women are born with: the ability and sensitivity to interpret personal and social complexities; the capacity to nurture; the aptitude for insight and obviously, the gift of female intuition. Also, women have the remarkable ability to produce a 10-carat diamond in much the same way that nature does—by putting a man under terrific pressure.

However, women should not feel overly smug about their genetic superiority since men have always been the dominant sex and it is not likely that this fact will change—if for no other reason than *basic physical strength*. Consider, for example, what happens when a group of lions comes upon a herd of elk. It's possible that the elk may be genetically superior to the lion, however, when the lion outruns the elk and seizes it by the throat, genetic superiority is probably the last thing on the elk's mind.

Even though the human male may be a domesticated animal, the combination of superior physical strength and the basic instinct to conquer gives him the dominant edge over the female—rendering her vulnerable to rape and physical abuse, a fear that every woman has to some degree or another.

At what age does a child become aware of his or her sexuality?

Usually by age four or five. And coincidentally, that's the age when a little girl's femininity becomes "attractive" to grown males. This, of course, does not go unnoticed by the little girl as she quickly learns that she can definitely get more from her daddy by being cute and cuddly, than she can from her mother with the same behavior. Little girls can develop modes of behavior that turn their fathers, literally, into *sugar daddies.*

A little boy's masculinity at age four or five, however, is normally not "attractive" to grown females, so the little boy has somewhat of a disadvantage in this area; nevertheless, he'll catch up in during his teen years when his masculinity will definitely become "attractive" to grown females. At that time, young boys learn how to extract reassurances from their mothers to build their confidence and male egos.

Puberty for a girl is a dramatic time-marked event, centered around the onset of her menstruation. For a boy, puberty is far more gradual and seamless—more like a slowly developing series of events.

Can a girl in her early teens actually "encourage" an affair with a much older man?

Unfortunately, yes, but it's usually not a *conscious* effort on the girl's part—to begin with.

The initial expression of sexual interest from an older man may at first arouse fear in a young girl. She is, at this point, a "victim" being pursued by an unknown force. At the same time, however, the desires expressed by the older man can awaken and stimulate her own emerging sexual awareness. Along with her fear of the unknown, the girl will feel flattered at first and if the man is persistent in his show of affection and the girl's fascination with sexual experimentation overrides her fear, she will soon begin to sense the power that her sexual attraction holds and feel the need to explore this newly discovered power. Eventually, she will be a willing participant.

If the affair is continued over an extended period of time, very often, the older man becomes the victim—being enslaved to the young girl's increasing sexual control over him and his fear of losing her to a younger man.

Freud would call this scenario an enactment of the Electra—commonly known as Oedipus—complex, where the daughter *unconsciously* desires to win her father. No matter how the relationship is labeled, it's an unhealthy situation for all concerned—and nobody can emerge a winner.

Will young girls today be more content with themselves as adults than women are today?

In the majority of cases, yes.

A lot of *battles* have been fought and won over the last twenty to thirty years and a lot has been learned from trial and error. One such example was the attempt by toy companies to battle gender gap in youth by establishing gender neutrality in their products; i.e., "same-sex" toys. Unfortunately, they didn't sell. Subsequent marketing research revealed the obvious: little girls are not the same as little boys—they want toys that appeal to their basic instincts of femininity and masculinity. Girls have definitely made progress in narrowing the gender gap when it comes to sports activities and academic pursuits in math and science. Young girls today have a great deal more freedom to pursue their interests, they have gained a sense of autonomy and therefore, are getting a better shot at realizing long term goals.

Individual parental and family values, of course, have tremendous impact on a young child. Choice of projects and outside activities plays a large part in a child's developing identity.

Do men resent the control their mothers had over their lives?

Most do, unconsciously, if not consciously. Even in the most "well-adjusted" men, you'll detect an underlying element of resentment, and usually, guilt.

Long-standing traditional systems of belief inevitably shape future attitudes. For example, little boys instinctively begin life loving their mothers and showing obvious signs of affection. As teenagers, however, they are pressured to abandon this behavior since society discourages young men from any conduct that might be considered soft and feminine.

If a woman is thinking seriously about getting involved with a man and wonders whether the love they feel for each other will grow, she doesn't need a crystal ball. All she has to do is examine his present relationship with his mother. If she sees that he has a strong resentment for the mother, he will eventually transfer those negative feelings to the wife. Or, if he has intense guilt feelings about his mother, this can be a web that will continue to be woven around any woman in the man's life. Guilt is something that lingers, crawling along in the mind like a spider on a never-ending thread of his own spinning.

It's important to remember that there is an unconscious if not conscious struggle for power in *every* relationship— even the healthiest—so it certainly makes sense to team up with someone who doesn't come to you with a built-in resentment that keeps you off balance like a tightrope walker with an itch.

Are men ever free of their mother's control?

Almost never. The effect of a mother's control will always be with a man, in varying degrees and her influence will be carried over in his relationships with other women. For instance, if a man had a conflicted and dependent relationship with a female figure when he was young (his mother, grandmother, etc.), the unconscious "seeds" of this conflicted relationship will resurface and plant themselves firmly in any adult relationship with a woman, regardless of who she is.

Consider the case of Jonathan—an intelligent, successful physician who—by all appearances—seemed to have everything. When Jonathan's relationship with Sandra—also a physician—looked like it was heading for a professional as well as a marital partnership, Jonathan's mother appeared on the scene. Very soon after that, Jonathan disappeared. Apparently, Jonathan was capable only of dating women on a casual basis. When it came to commitment, his heart belonged to mother.

Why do men feel they have to act tough?

Because that's the most popular definition of masculinity. "Tough guys" like John Wayne and Humphrey Bogart have always been considered the ultimate of the male heroes; and of course sports figures are continually revered for their rough and tumble aggressiveness. Little boys today clamor for action figure toys, in an effort to live out their inexhaustible fantasies of being just like the action heroes they see on film.

Outside of the movies and sports arenas—in the offices and routine work world—the image persists. Men are expected—and expect themselves—to be tough. When it comes to personal relationships, however, many men are resistant to dropping the "tough guy" image and showing a "soft" side. In too many cases, it's only a facade to disguise their own fears.

For example, a man may love and need a woman, but he'll be afraid of her at the same time. He'll worry that he might disappoint her, that he might lose her love, or worse yet, that she'll abandon him. The easiest way to disguise these fears and insecurities is to hide them behind the gritty and gutsy exterior of the tough guy.

Why is a woman criticized when she wants to be—or has to be—tough?

It's strictly a matter of tradition. For so many centuries, women were supposed to be seen and not heard.

Today, however, women are not only seen and heard, they're in your face! Men just aren't used to that kind of behavior and in many cases, don't *want* to get used to it. Additionally, there are some women who do not accept this kind of behavior in other women.

The best cure, of course, for this paradox is time—since stereotypes take a long time to go away. Eventually, being tough" will be a behavioral choice for women just as it is for men. Until that happens, however, women area going to feel like they're crossing the desert on a pogo stick.

Do men resent the power that women have when it comes to sex?

Definitely. But resentment of a woman's power isn't confined to just sex. Men spend just about *all* of their lives under a woman's control; think of the little boy who feels *only* as strong as the reflection he sees in his mother's eyes.

Then, when the little boy reaches adulthood and flees the nest to freedom, he finds himself once again under the control of females as he explores the sexual side of his life.

When the adult male decides to marry, the extent of a woman's power over his life increases; not only does the wife maintain clout when it comes to sex, the man will once again feel only as strong as the reflection he sees—now—in his wife's eyes.

Is it any wonder then that men harbor fantasies of sexual dominance and power, such as secretly wanting to be a bouncer in a brothel?

Will women always be perceived as sex objects?

Yes—to a greater or lesser degree—depending upon the century in which you live. A man's basic primary sexual instinct has always been and always will be to conquer. It's not going to go away!

Females, over the centuries, have been both used and abused as sex objects. Consider the old quotation that is still around: *"The debauching of virgins and the amours of strumpets will always be the subjects of comedy."* Today, jokes about prostitutes and virgins fill the television and movie screens, are categorized in joke pages on the Internet and are considered staples in a stand-up comic's routine.

Only recently in civilized societies, have women *aggressively* fought against the concept of their physical bodies being seen as purely sexual and refused to be slaves to their gender. Trying to *eliminate* this concept, however, is pretty much like trying to get molasses to flow uphill.

Are we still laboring under a double standard?

In many areas, yes. Today, little girls as well as little boys are raised in a more sexually free and easy environment. This 'across the board' freedom, however, leaves girls far more vulnerable because they now lack the heretofore built-in protective shield of shyness and fear.

For example, If a teenage girl becomes pregnant, society turns against her and condemns her for the results of the very sexual behavior that today's society condones. Once pregnant, she is still treated as an outcast; however, the teenage boy who fathers a child, suffers little or nothing by comparison.

In the adult world, penile implants—costing between $12,000 and $15,000—is covered by Medicare; breast augmentation is not. Medicaid, the federal insurance program for the poor and disabled, pays for the new male impotence drug, Viagra; however, it *does not* cover infertility treatments or birth control for women.

Since difference, by its very existence, invites competition it's apparent that the shadings of our double standard will continually *change* with time—but it is foolish to think that a single standard can ever exist.

What are the most recent shifts in the double standard?

The most notable are the increased level of women's independence, their freedom to pursue individual goals, plus more recognition and somewhat improved financial gain in the workplace. However research of the Fortune 500 companies shows that women are still having difficulty advancing their careers and remain pretty much invisible in the corner offices.

One area that reflects a blending of the standards is the world of youth and beauty. In an effort to be desirable, women have spent fortunes on makeup and beauty salons; put hot wax on their skins, ripped out hair by the roots; starved their bodies, strapped themselves into torture machines to stay firm; then run to the plastic surgeon to cut, lift, snip, clip, peel, prune, lop off, pull up and suck out.

Now, men are joining the ranks—going to beauty salons, exercising in health spas and seeking out plastic surgeons.

Are men really insensitive?

That seems to be the consensus among women in general. The truth is: men *do* have feelings—they just don't use them!

There appears to be an innate lack of ability and/or a lack of desire on the part of men to share their feelings or express themselves verbally. Furthermore, men don't really talk *with* each other. They talk *to* each other—about sports, about business or about politics. But that's where the line is drawn. Problems, sensitivities or personal doubts are definitely out of bounds in a male conversation—even with the best of buddies.

Feelings and emotions come naturally to women. With men, you have to scratch the surface, then dig around to find what's there. Unfortunately, most of the time, it's like plowing the sands.

CHAPTER THREE

"MEN AS CHATTEL—

OR MEN AS CHAMPIONS"

*I*T WAS MOLIERE'S *belief that,* **"Whatever people may say, the great ambition of women is to inspire love."** *In this modern, new-millennium world, do Moliere's words still ring true?*

Women today have more freedom than ever before, but freedom can be frightening. Aside from relationships, there are jobs, careers, professions, financial opportunities, travel, sports, hobbies and creative pursuits. The choices are as endless as the line in a circle.

If life changes and instincts don't, what happens?

* * *

What is the psychological basis for a man's need to dominate?

A man begins his existence as a defenseless and impotent being, completely dependent upon a woman's body and a woman's nurturing.

As he matures and develops, his goal is to reverse this order so that he is the one who has the control and superiority over a woman. This is an internal battle he will wage all of his life.

Do women need love in their lives?

Everybody needs love. In an effort to show their "independence," some women try to deny the fact that they need love, but those who are true to themselves know that this is a very basic part of a woman's nature.

Women are at their best when they have a love to stimulate them and drive them.

Basically, women have an innate, *natural* need to perform or work for the "benefit" of someone they love. The object of their love could be a man, a woman, a child, a boss or even a pet.

Can a woman be happy with OR without a man?

Of course, but the choice must be *hers.*

Not every woman will find "Mr. Right," nor will every man find "Ms. Right." Since this is not a perfect world and very few people achieve fulfillment of every need, the only intelligent approach is to aim for what you want, embrace what you can get and adjust to what you can't have.

A woman today has options: to be with a man, to be with another woman, or to be alone. We are all aware of the old maid character in gothic novels who has her hair knotted tightly in a bun and her lace collar securely closed around her neck, hiding away from the rest of the world because she is unmarried. Today, when a woman is secure in her own identity, she doesn't have to be ashamed because she doesn't have a husband , nor does today's woman have to spend all of her energies plotting to *catch* a man—unless she's decided that's what she wants to do.

Thankfully, now, the pursuit of a woman's happiness is her own choice.

Can a woman consider a man only as an "asset" when establishing a relationship?

Of course, if that is what she wants. There certainly are times when a woman would love to have a good-looking man on her arm when she walks into a room, or have a particularly influential man escort her to an important or high-profile function. She may view these men as "temporary" or, in some cases, consider them a "necessity" to make an impression or to further her career. Why not?

For centuries, men have had the freedom to love as well as like women and they also had the freedom to deal with women as chattel. So, now that women have the freedom to love as well as like men, why not treat men as chattel when it pleases them?

Should a woman use her sexuality and femininity to control a man?

You bet—every opportunity she can! The best way to accomplish this, of course, is to let the man think that *he* is still the master of his own fate.

It's really quite basic: when a woman understands that a man has an instinctive *hunger* to conquer and to feel powerful, she can use her femininity and sexuality to *feed* those instincts. Men are simple creatures who basically look to find themselves in women. Men want reassurance that they are masculine and that they are important. A woman should be generous in her praise, show her admiration of his accomplishments and most effective of all, make him feel strong by showing him she needs him.

Even if a man is aware that he's playing by the woman's rules, he'll love the game anyway because *it satisfies his masculine instincts*, builds his self image and when you tally up the score, both he and the woman are winners.

It's pretty self defeating for women to "flaunt" their independence by running around shouting into men's faces that women are superior to men. That may be true, but it's a detail that should stay out of sight or it will ruin the game.

A woman does have some powerful "tools." It's a shame to let them go to waste. Consider the example of Theresa, age 40, and Tommy, age 26, who decided to start an auto repair business together, as equal partners. Tommy had worked for Teresa's father as an auto repairman for several years before her father decided to retire. Teresa was married to an accountant and had two children in college.

After about one year of working closely together and fighting constantly, Teresa was tempted to sever the partnership with Tommy. But she hated to give up, especially since they were just beginning to make a profit and future prospects for growth looked promising.

Teresa decided she'd ask her mother if she had any ideas on how to remedy the situation. Her mother had just one suggestion: start treating Tommy like a man as well as a partner.

The pieces of the puzzle started falling into place. Teresa began to realize that she had been so intent on proving she could work just as hard as a man, she had lost sight of the fact that her efforts to do everything as well or better than Tommy, had robbed him of his need to feel masculine in her eyes. His reaction to this *insult,* of course was irritability and anger.

Teresa decided it was time to use a few of her own female *tools* to do some repairs. The next time she had something heavy to lift, instead of straining and trying to do it herself, she walked over to Tommy and told him that the box was too heavy for her. She asked him if he would handle it for her, since he was stronger. Naturally, he jumped at the chance to show off his strength.

Teresa quickly discovered that her feminine instincts would be her most valuable *tools* in making the repair business with Tommy a success.

"Helping a damsel in distress" is the best thing that can happen to a man in any relationship—personal or professional. He'll love coming to the rescue, being needed, and feeling tough and protective.

Insecure women may feel that appearing helpless is a compromise to their gender or may rationalize that they don't want to "play games." The truth is, however, that there is a striking difference between *games* and *negotiation*.

Secure women are happily aware of the fact that using their femininity is as essential to their existence as applause is to an actor. Of course, an actor can live without applause, but it's certainly not very rewarding.

Is it necessary to play hard to get when you're interested in a man?

It helps. Men like to pursue and the more elusive the woman is, the more challenging it is—pretty much like going after a slippery bar of soap in the bathtub.

Above all, men like to conquer and it's definitely a mistake to make the conquest easy. Some of the wealthiest men in the world "buy" beautiful women to stay by their sides, then let them go when they're tired of them. But the women they worship—the women they would absolutely sell their kingdoms for—are the ones whose love they *cannot* buy.

What is the best way to attract a man's attention?

Flirting. And, frankly, it's a lost art.

Flirting is fun and it's a wonderful and *safe* way of showing a man you're interested in him. Even the strongest man will melt under the heat of flattery.

The best way to flirt is with your eyes. When you smile and fix your gaze on a man, he'll know you're interested. If he smiles and returns the gaze, you're on your way. If he doesn't, move on.

The tone of your voice is as important as what you say; keep it soft. And, of course, body language tells a lot about how you feel. If you're open to the idea of knowing a man, face him directly. Don't turn to the side or back away from him. If you're seated together and talking, lean forward as if you're intent on hearing his every word.

Despite the "tough" facade, most men fear rejection when it comes to getting to know a woman. Flirting is a subtle and appealing way to encourage them.

Why do some men say they like "bitchy" women?

It's important to understand that a man's definition of "bitchy" is very different than a woman's definition.

"Bitchy" to a man means a woman who is not passive—someone who is *devilish* or *playfully* aggressive. To many men, this "bitchy" kind of woman represents a challenge. These men want the ego rush of conquering them.

What a man really *does not* want is someone who nags, whines, is insensitive and/or verbally castrating—the definition that most women use for the word, "bitchy."

Are there early warning signs a woman can spot that will give her insight into a man BEFORE she gets too involved?

Definitely. If a woman has invested the effort to know and understand herself, one of the rewards of her investment will be the ability to understand more about other people.

Men will give you all the information you'll ever need if you stay with reality and not be blinded by *what you'd like that person to be.* Keep your eyes and ears connected to your instincts and intuition, then watch and listen.

Start by checking out his physical appearance. For example, is he neat and well groomed? Are his clothes proper to the occasion? Are his shoes worn out or is the shoe style extreme? Does he have an appropriate haircut?

Look carefully at his facial features. Does he look at you when he talks or does he shift his eyes away? Is his mouth relaxed? Does he grin inappropriately?

Check out his mannerisms. Does he show any feminine traits when he walks or the way he stands? Does he constantly display nervous gestures with his hands, such as picking at his cuticles or fingernails or repeatedly clenching his fists? If you sense negative responses in yourself to anything you see or hear, pay attention. Carefully examine the extent or depth of what you feel and don't compromise your standards. "Red flags" are easy to spot if you're not color blind.

For instance, say you make a dinner date with a man to go out to an elegant French restaurant that you *both* have heard about—and he shows up at your door dressed in faded jeans, sneakers, and a plaid shirt that might or might not have a stain on the front.

If you observe inappropriate behavior in someone, it's like finding a snag in your pantyhose. Sooner or later, it's going to run the whole length, so you better change fast.

What about warning signs later in a relationship?

A lot of the clues you see once a relationship gets "comfort-able" are excellent indicators, not only of a man's personality and character, but they should serve as a mini-preview of what life would be like if you spent your future with him. (Don't forget, as a woman gaining insight into yourself, you should also be aware of the personality and character traits that *you* will carry into the future.)

One area that is especially sensitive to many women is personal grooming. It's rather obvious that men quickly de-teriorate without razors and clean clothes—pretty much like potted plants that go to seed unless they're pruned and wa-tered. So, if you see that a man has a tendency to go *natural* and look like someone who's spent the night in a bus station, consider what your future is going to hold.

Another good testing ground for warning signs can be seen at the dining table. Eating a meal with a man can ex-pose some important revelations about his personality, his character and also, his sexual habits. For instance, check to see if his table manners are sloppy or if he chews with his mouth open. If it offends you on the first or second date, think how you'll feel after many years of sitting across the table from him. You won't be able to avoid the problem by rearranging your chairs, because sooner or later, an impor-tant business contact you want to impress might be seated opposite the man of your dreams at a dinner party.

Another warning bell that could sound an alarm: If he can't decide what to order and continually vacillates in his selection, chances are that his indecisiveness cuts a wide swath throughout his personality—including his sexual technique.

Also, if he orders the least expensive items on the menu and reacts negatively if you order something expensive, you should consider excusing yourself to go to the restroom and leave by the back door. (Always remember to carry cash or credit cards for just such emergencies.)

Cheapness is an unpleasant trait that will pop up everywhere like a rash. It will affect relationships with friends and family, in business and especially in bed. If a man cannot be generous in his everyday actions, how can he be generous with his sexual behavior?

Other warning signs to watch for include: drinking habits, the way a man drives, if he keeps his car in good shape, how he treats animals, and if he displays aggressive or inappropriate behavior.

The one thing to always remember when evaluating someone: *people grow more like themselves as they grow older.*

Why are older men often attracted to younger women?

Youth and beauty can be strong magnets and it's normal for an older man to occasionally feel the pull. In most cases, however, it's just a temporary enticement—very much like the appeal of a squirrel to an apartment-bred dog who's been told to stay.

When an older man does decide to bolt and run—divorcing his older mate and marrying a much younger woman—he is desperately trying to re-claim his youth. He feels that the best way to reassure himself that he is still potent is by winning a *trophy* and displaying her for all to see.

Most of these marriages, if they last, are destined for escalating problems. As the older man gets even older, his lifestyle will become more sedentary; he will want to simplify his life and do less. About that time, however, the young wife will just be hitting her stride and want to conduct her life at a faster pace than her stay-at-home husband. The best that can be hoped for in this situation is compromise on both sides which, of course, cannot always be easily accomplished.

Why is it uncommon to see older women with younger men?

Because women usually do not feel they have to reaffirm their sexual prowess as they get older, in the way that men do.

Women, of course, never outgrow their need to feel attractive to men but this compulsion is not as compelling as the pressures a man feels when he senses he's losing his sexual potency.

What should a woman do when her professional success threatens a man in whom she's interested?

Men *instinctively* want to be the conquering heroes. So when a man looks at a successful, independent woman, he sees someone who doesn't need the very thing he wants to give her: *his strength and protection.*

However, all is not lost, because a woman has the ability—if she chooses—to *change* what the man sees.

Consider the story of Catherine and Phillip: Catherine was a prosperous businesswoman with her own investment agency. Phillip was a brilliant engineer who was struggling to move ahead in his career by trying to patent one of his inventions. After several dates, Catherine was hooked. She knew that Phillip was the right man for her, but she also sensed that Phillip was holding back. He appeared to be intimidated by his "lack of accomplishment" compared to hers. He brought up the subject alot. Catherine always responded by saying that "all of that didn't mean anything" and that she admired him for what and who he was. Somehow, Phillip never reacted like he believed her.

Time passed and the relationship stagnated. Eventually Phillip broke off their friendship. Six months later, Catherine learned that he had become engaged to a successful and well-respected trial lawyer. Catherine was devastated. When Phillip left her, she had consoled herself by saying that it was "probably for the best" and that he would be better off with a woman who was less intimidating.

How wrong she was. As Catherine would come to understand later, she lost Phillip because she failed to let her femininity show through and encourage his masculinity to come out. She didn't have to change who or what she was; all she had to do was *shift the emphasis.*

For instance, instead of insisting on paying the check every time they went out to dinner—even though Phillip would protest vigorously—Catherine should have allowed him to pay and not tried to convince him that it made more sense for her to pay since he was struggling financially and needed to be conservative. Basically, Catherine was intent on filling her own needs and failing to recognize Phillip's.

When Catherine moved to a new apartment, she should have allowed Phillip to help her move, but, instead, Catherine turned down his offer and insisted that Phillip shouldn't waste his valuable time. She told him it would be easier for her to hire movers to do it all.

It's obvious that Phillip enjoyed the company of intelligent women—but not at the expense of his masculinity—a fact that Catherine failed to see. The lawyer, on the other hand, apparently understood herself well enough to shift the emphasis away from her own needs and over to Phillip's.

Do men find it difficult to relate to a woman who is both intelligent and attractive?

It all depends upon the man's level of security in his own manhood.

There are some men who can tolerate only one or the other of these qualities in a woman.

If a man is uncertain about his own abilities and accomplishments and feels threatened by female intelligence, he'll avoid it and narrow his search to women whose major attribute is physical beauty. If a man is insecure about his masculinity and overwhelmed by the sexual power of attractive women—fearing he will lose control and become engulfed—he will seek refuge in the company of more intelligent females whose physical beauty does not pose a threat to him.

There are some women who are known for being hard, tough and totally independent—then suddenly, they find themselves being soft and feminine. Why does this happen?

Because "someone" entered that woman's life and precipitated the change.

Strength and independence are qualities that surface in response to outside forces such as challenges and adversity. The degree of strength and independence, of course, depends upon an individual's character, personality, heredity, etc.

Softness and femininity are mostly *instinctive* responses. An individual may try to "hide" these instincts, however, they are like mercury and will definitely "surface" when stimulated.

If the *right* person enters a strong and independent woman's life and triggers those soft and feminine instincts, she'll soon discover the many "rewards" of being a multi-dimensional woman.

Why do some women feel that they are betraying the feminist cause if they behave soft and feminine?

There is no reason other than societal pressure—which, of course, is a foolish reason to deny one's self the pleasure of enjoying womanhood. It's difficult enough being a woman in a man's world—why not take full advantage of what is rightfully yours? It's called, being feminine without apology.

One of the more exceptional *tools* we have as women is

the ability to tap into our emotions, bring them to the surface and allow them to grow. A woman can have it all—strength, independence *and* femininity. Overruling one's instincts in the name of some fickle feminist flag is an inglorious form of *self* betrayal.

Should a woman feel ashamed if she has spent the majority of her life in a man's shadow?

She should stay right there and not budge an inch—*as long as she's happy.* If a man throws a long shadow and if a woman likes the shade, who's to judge?

Shadows can be very cool.

CHAPTER FOUR

"CHOICES AND CHALLENGES—

WHEN YOU'RE NOT ATTRACTED

TO THE OPPOSITE SEX"

*S*OME MATTERS INTRODUCE *themselves into a person's life on their own terms and not on yours. When this happens, you have two choices: respond to the inevitable or turn a deaf ear.*

Turning a deaf ear, of course, is pretty much like the piano player in a bordello denying the fact that anything is going on upstairs.

* * *

Is every person born with a homosexual/bisexual potential?

The jury is still out on that question. Biological, physiological, sociological and psychological evidence continues to mount on all sides, but no definitive conclusions have yet to be substantiated.

The one thing we do know is that men and women need *both* male and female hormones to function normally. We don't know if an endocrine variance in the brain contributes to alternate sexuality choices or how much psychological and environmental factors influence sexuality.

There are also individuals who are so uncomfortable with their own biological gender, they feel compelled to "change" completely to the opposite sex. This appears to be more common in men than in women. Traditionally, a man who feels that he was truly meant to be a woman—but is trapped in a man's body—has experienced this desire since early childhood and will dress in women's clothes whenever possible. Considering himself as trans-sexual or transgendered—*not* gay—he will take hormone treatments, use electrolysis or other permanent hair removal systems and finally, undergo surgery in an effort to *totally* convert.

Due to the significant advances in plastic surgery in recent times, the results of a sex-change operation can be quite remarkable. The expense, of course, is high, but the mental as well as the physical rewards appear to be well worth it.

The origin of an individual's sexuality may someday be confined to a single explanation. But until that time occurs, it is important that men and women today understand and feel comfortable with their own individual sexual identity no matter what the origin.

What should a woman do when she's ambivalent about her sexual orientation?

Analyze every doubt and investigate every instinct like a lawyer building a case. Introspection is never easy—it takes strength to pursue the questions and courage to face the answers—but it's always productive.

This story about Felicia is a good illustration: As a young student in a strange city, Felicia welcomed the offers of help from Lorraine, an older graduate student. At first, they would see each other only occasionally, but it wasn't long before brief encounters evolved into extended evenings, then weekends together at a rented lake cottage. After several months, Lorraine asked Felicia to move into her apartment and live with her. Felicia agreed.

Felicia had never acknowledged the possibility that she might be a lesbian. Whenever the thought crossed her mind, she would quickly discard it, telling herself that she was just slow in ripening. She rationalized that she had no real sexual experience and that sooner or later everything would sort itself out.

Being with Lorraine seemed "natural" so Felicia allowed herself the complacency of letting the relationship *happen* to her. Any misgivings or reluctance she felt were quickly eased away by Lorraine's reassurances.

Their relationship grew more and more comfortable with time. Felicia went on to graduate school and Lorraine took a job in the marketing department of a large hotel chain. Then something began to stir within Felicia that she couldn't ignore. She admitted to herself that, obviously, she had lesbian tendencies, but was she *truly* a lesbian? She didn't really have any experience with men and knew that she didn't find men particularly appealing, but how could she be sure until she tried?

Felicia attempted to discuss her feelings with Lorraine, but Lorraine made light of the subject and told Felicia that she was being silly—that it was obvious she was a lesbian and that she should just accept it and conduct her life accordingly.

The doubts continued to plague Felicia, growing to the point where she knew she had to make a decision. Three months later, Felicia moved into a small apartment of her own. Lorraine was devastated, but Felicia was determined to find some answers and told Lorraine that it was best they didn't see each other any more.

Felicia concentrated all her energies on her studies, preparing for graduation and an eventual teaching position at the university. There were many evenings she felt alone and confused, but she trusted her instincts and knew that the only way she would ever understand herself totally would be to leave the door open and deal with whatever came through.

It wasn't long before Marvin strolled right in. He was a fellow graduate student that Felicia had known casually for several years. One day, as they both were leaving a lecture, Marvin asked Felicia to join him for coffee. He confided in her that his wife had left him and was planning to marry another man. He told Felicia that he desperately needed someone to talk to and she appeared to be such an understanding person. Felicia assured him that she would be glad to be his friend and help him in any way she could.

The following week, Felicia joined Marvin for dinner. He was feeling very sad and didn't want to be alone. Felicia was attentive and compassionate but when she tried to bring the evening to a close, Marvin reacted badly. He seemed very upset and asked Felicia if he could go back to her apartment with her and stay just for a little while. Felicia found it impossible to turn him down.

Once inside her apartment, Marvin moved close to Felicia, holding her face gently cupped in his hands like someone thirsty gathering water. She didn't resist as he kissed her. She remembers thinking at that moment that she felt no sexual stirring but she felt an enormous curiosity.

Their affair lasted one month and the parting was amicable. Marvin found someone else and Felicia found an answer—which turned out to be more of a milestone.

On the night Marvin left, Felicia started a diary. The first line read, *"My future is about to begin."* The next page almost wrote itself:

> *"Making love with a woman, then making love with a man, is like placing a piece of white lace on dark velvet. I see now what I couldn't see before.*
>
> *I have discovered that my nature is meant to thrive in the light of a woman's tenderness and sensitivity—like a flower leaning toward the sun. I realize by my responses that I cannot give a man what he needs and he cannot give me what I need."*

Felicia graduated and began her teaching career. In time, she met an attorney named Sarah and a year later, they bought a home together and started plans to adopt a baby.

Would a relationship between two women have less interpersonal obstacles than a relationship between a man and a woman?

On a basic level, yes—in the same way that two people speaking English communicate better than if one of them speaks a foreign language.

Usually, the lesbian lifestyle leads to quicker relationships since women tend to be more emotional and sensitive in their involvements.

Gay men, on the other hand, tend to seek out sexual involvements long before establishing an emotional bond and making a commitment with one individual.

Would a lesbian marriage have a greater or lesser chance of survival than a heterosexual marriage?

In today's world, the chances of finding success in *any* marriage is pretty much like locating a taxi in the rain. Some people do it, but it takes a little luck and a lot of patience.

Homosexual partners have the added challenge of having to establish their own marital guidelines since they don't have the benefit of long-standing, pre-set patterns and comfortable traditions to ease the adjustment of their union. Every relationship, of course, can survive the test of time if it is fueled by communication, dedication and personal sacrifice.

Was homosexuality ever accepted as normal?

Hundreds of years ago in Greece—when women had no more value than an animal—male homosexuality was considered not only normal, but *superior* to heterosexuality, since sexual relations with another man obviously had more merit than sexual relations with an inferior "creature." Additionally, lesbianism was quite common during this same period as women gravitated to one another as a way to escape their enslavement and rejection.

Is it likely homosexuality will be accepted as normal again?

If history is any guide, it certainly is possible. In fact, our present culture reflects an increasingly successful assimilation of gay people into areas of business, politics, education and religion—as well as culture and entertainment.

Homosexuality, heterosexuality and bisexuality all have flourished during one period or another in history, depending upon the social climate and conditions of the times. In a setting that is built on the foundation of male dominance and strong family traditions, heterosexuality seems to be the norm.

When did the acceptance of homosexuality begin its rise to the level that we know today?

In the late 1960's and early1970's. During this period, the voice of the women's movement—and an outcry for personal freedom—was echoing throughout the country. Homosexuality emerged from the darkness like a train coming out of a tunnel.

The voice of the gay culture was heard loud and clear when it publically announced its presence as an alternative lifestyle. The line was drawn for all to see between homosexuality and heterosexuality and the boundaries were set. In the early 1970's, the American Psychiatric Association eliminated homosexuality from its roster of mental illnesses.

Are gay men more tolerant of lesbians than heterosexual men?

As a general rule, no.

Unfortunately, male chauvinism can be felt in both the homosexual and heterosexual worlds.

Why do so many single women say that gay men are the best escorts?

There are many reasons. When a woman is out on a "date" with a gay man, she can completely relax and enjoy their shared interests. It's so much easier because there are no sexual pressures to deal with and no worries about whether to get involved or not involved. The man is *totally* available to her as a person and she can literally be herself.

Julia and Paul are good examples: Julia is a recently divorced, mature woman who is active in the arts community in New York City and her dear friend, Paul, is an actor who is gay. They have known each other for many years.

During Julia's divorce, Paul proved to be one of her most important mainstays of support. They regularly had dinner together to discuss the emotional difficulties she was dealing with. Paul proved to be a wonderful sounding board and was immensely understanding and consoling.

Now that Julia is free and on her own again, she continues to have dinner with Paul on a regular basis. This time around, however, their discussions are more likely to center on who has the newest love affair. And when the weather permits, *both* Paul and Julia can be seen admiring men as they stroll together down Fifth Avenue.

Why are some heterosexuals paranoid about homosexuals while others are very accepting?

Psychologists and psychiatrists seem to agree that extreme paranoia about homosexuality usually stems from a person's *own* unconscious fears of his or her *latent* homosexual tendencies. In other words, a person who has recoiled from any sign of latent tendencies within himself, will be totally unnerved by contact with a homosexual, since this contact will invariably "hit a nerve" and force these tendencies to surface again.

Some people are so fanatical in their fear and hate of homosexuals, they feel safe only when they are hiding behind religious dogma—such as the man who espoused the theory that "If God had meant us to have homosexuals, he would have created Adam and Bruce."

There is a relatively "mild," general dislike of homosexuality that can occasionally be felt, but that is due mostly to a fear of the unknown. Since the boundaries of sexual preference have been more openly defined and the characteristics of alternative lifestyles are clearly evident—not only in the media and entertainment worlds, but in everyday life as well—heterosexuals seem to be increasingly more comfortable and more accepting of homosexuality.

In the past, for example, when the boundaries were blurred, even a heterosexual man who felt the need to step outside of the usual confines of "social" behavior by growing his hair long and wearing jewelry, ran the risk of being labeled a homosexual. Now that alternative lifestyles are more clearly defined, people can feel less limited in their behavior.

Obviously, if we lived in an ideal world, it would be unheard of to evaluate an individual by his sexual preference instead of defining him or her as a whole human being.

Why do gay men appear to have an easier time "fitting in" to society than lesbians do?

Because of the undeniable fact that we live in a male dominated society. *All* females, regardless of their individual pursuits, their professional goals, or their sexual orientation, are coming from behind in the race for equality.

Women, however, do appear to have more "choice" than men do when it comes to sexual orientation. Lesbian women are more comfortable moving from dating men to dating women, then back to dating men, if they so choose. Gay men rarely show that kind of "flexibility." Perhaps this difference is due to the *natural* inclination of women to establish close emotional ties to other women no matter what their orientation.

Can you enjoy being a woman if you're a lesbian?

Of course. Some say, *twice as much*!

CHAPTER FIVE

"STAYING SINGLE—

A FREE SPIRIT OR A MATCH UNLIT?

*I*T USED TO *be that a woman's goal was to get married as soon as possible and a man's was to stay unmarried as long as he could. Today, however, marital status is as fickle as shifts in the wind. It's no longer a choice of either/or—it's a matter of which direction you choose.*

Single people can live alone and develop careers or they can live together: men with women, men with men and women with women. Married people can get divorced, stay single, get married again and repeat the process as often as they want. Single people can choose to never marry, then become parents through adoption or selected fertilization.

* * *

How can a single women establish her own identity in a couple's world?

By devoting her efforts to learning about herself and discovering what she is capable of accomplishing. No one's identity should be dependent upon being part of a couple—even if they are married or living with someone.

Every woman, single or married, can lead a full, active and rewarding life—but it's something she must create herself through work, outside interests and hobbies or by involvement with charities. Once a woman gains self esteem and confidence, she will be better equipped to resist any temptation to compromise her standards or withstand any pressure to rationalize away her *real* needs for the sake of fitting into a "role." People who make life *happen to them* are by far the most intriguing people and always have the most stimulating friends.

It's true that "no one is an island." However, living alone doesn't mean that you *are* alone. For instance, you can have a man in your life—but *not necessarily* in your house.

Is there a risk to becoming selfish when you're single?

There is a very definite tendency for single people to develop their own *private* meanings to life. It depends upon the person, of course, but single people—by the nature of their daily lives and the fact that there's not a built-in *requirement* to share—tend to develop "tunnel vision" when it comes to their sense of responsibility to people around them.

When interests stay centered on individual and materialistic needs, eventually a person will measure successes and achievements in terms of personal superiority, rather than seeking fellowship and cooperation with others to achieve more meaningful goals.

Why are there so many women in their 30's and 40's still single?

The "popular" answer to this question is career demands. In reality, however, there is another rather significant determinant: Most young woman today are not willing to *settle* for less than what they really want—not only in their choice of a career, but also, in their choice of a mate.

Women, today, basically expect more from themselves *and* from others. Therefore, the level of achievement will naturally be directly proportional to the level of expectation.

Career satisfaction, financial security and independence are achievements a woman can accomplish *herself,* so why settle for less when it comes to an important decision like marriage? Today's woman can afford to wait until the *right* person comes along. And if she wants a child, she certainly does not have to marry a man to have one.

Is there a trend toward women becoming single mothers?

Yes, in fact, It's becoming almost fashionable. Women are discovering that the luxury of having options is certainly superior to the sacrifices of compromise.

The number of single-mother adoptions is rising rapidly. Women are adopting newborns and young babies, not only in this country, but they are reaching out to other cultures worldwide for children.

Another product of this trend is the growth of sperm banks. Some women are discovering that the methodology of selection used at sperm banks can be superior to the *conventional* method of parenting—a fact that the animal kingdom has always known.

Consider the female of the species who seeks out—for reproduction purposes only—the healthiest, largest, strongest and most agile of the males. *The female animal has not fallen in love with the male, nor is she sitting around fantasiz-*

ing about their future together. Her only goal is to select the best genetically packaged male animal available to father her offspring. Once she's made her selection and the act is consummated, he's history. (There are obvious advantages to this agenda.)

The dynamics of the sperm banks are remarkably similar. Donors fill out lengthy 20 to 30 page profiles detailing personal information, social and cultural preferences, health history and a three-generation family history. Donors are thoroughly screened and tested medically—plus audiotapes of the donor's voice are made available.

A women seeking a donor to father her child reviews the profiles, then selects the precise characteristics she desires. For example, she may prefer a man with dark hair and blue eyes; someone who has advanced education and proven athletic ability. She can check his family history carefully to eliminate as much genetic risk as possible.

Furthermore, once a woman selects her donor, she can request that his additional sperm be stored for her in the future in case she wants her child to have a brother or sister by this same donor. (Even the animal kingdom hasn't figured that one out yet.)

Are some women better off staying single and never marrying?

Not *every* woman should be married. There are growing numbers of women who are single and delighted to stay that way. Some have been married briefly and divorced; some have never married at all. And contrary to popular belief, single women don't *hate* men. In fact, the majority of single women spend a good deal of time socializing with men as well as women.

The luxury of self indulgence and the satisfaction of "doing exactly what you want to do" is very appealing to some women. They consider the occasional feelings of loneliness a very small price to pay for their freedom.

Some mature women—who have spent the majority of their adult lives in a marriage that eventually ended in divorce or widowhood—express doubts when asked, "if they had to live their lives over again would they get married?"

One example is Sara: a bright woman and adventuresome by most standards. She left the security of a close family in a small town to "try her luck" in the big city when she was just 19 years old.

Sara got a job in a law firm doing clerical work and eight months later, married one of the young lawyers on the staff. Three years later, Sara found herself with two children and a husband who was working long hours to build his career.

Sara threw herself into the required wifely and motherly responsibilities even though she harbored a desire to return to college to get her degree. She discussed her ambition with her husband on several occasions, but he felt strongly that family demands were too great and that this should be a goal for Sarah to think about later, when the children were grown.

There were many times during the marriage when Sara's adventuresome nature would surface, but each time, her husband's "play it safe" nature prevailed: When birth control pills first entered the marketplace, Sara remembers asking her husband to buy just a small amount of stock in the drug company that was producing them. He refused, arguing that the pills would be too expensive for the average family and that the idea would never grow!

When the time came to buy a larger house for the family, Sara had her heart set on a beautiful older home on a small lake right in the heart of the city. Her husband agreed that the price was right, but that there were too many "risks" involved as far as the remodeling requirements. The family ended up in a "safe" traditional brick house that looked just like every other brick house on the street. Years later, the brick house sold for $300,000, but Sara's "dream house"—that had been bought and fixed up by another young couple—sold for $2,000,000.

Sara never achieved her goal of going back to college and getting her degree. After thirty years of marriage, Sara and her husband divorced. The lawyer that Sara chose to represent her, unfortunately was outwitted by her husband's law firm and Sara was left financially handicapped with minimal resources. Her children were grown and involved in their own lives. In reality, all Sara had left in her life to count on was Sara; she had few marketable skills and no financial security for the future. Sara had totally invested her adult life in others, sacrificing her personal goals and compromising her own fulfillment.

When she reflected on her life, Sara expressed no anger or hostility. She freely admitted that the choices she made were hers—that she could've "fought" for what she wanted, but it wasn't in "her nature" to do so. Considering the kind of woman she was and her need to explore life and "try new things," Sara felt strongly that if she could start all over again she would definitely *not* get married—no matter who the man was.

We all know that marriage provides *no* guarantees. By its very nature, marriage cannot be a solution to life's dilemmas, or a quick fix for seemingly unresolvable problems—even though society still considers marriage as the norm and single life to be less stable.

Was a woman better off in the past when she had a specified role?

A lot of woman would vote a resounding negative on that question, but there are a surprisingly large number of women who idealize the past. They feel that it was an "easier" way of life when men were the strong providers and women were safely tucked away at home and "taken care of."

One of the major stumbling blocks discovered in the women's liberation movement was their effort to "*unify*" all women. In hindsight, it became painfully obvious that women are extremely varied in their endeavors, their individual requirements and, above all, their personal desires.

There definitely are women who would adore to hear their husband say, "Darling, you just stay home and take it easy; I'll be the one to go out in the world and fight for what we need."

And then, of course, there's the modern millennium woman who juggles career, husband, children, nannies, social responsibilities and family pets—yet still has time to go the salon for a pedicure and bikini wax.

Will there be an increase in the number of single women who will regard men only as transient interludes in their lives as they get older?

There's no doubt about it. The group is swelling like bullfrogs at mating time. More women are deciding not to "settle" and to be patient until the "right" man comes along before getting married or making a long-term commitment.

It is true that patience is mostly the art of hoping, but on a day-to-day basis, hope alone provides a very lean diet. In the interim, short-term affairs can fulfill a woman's sexual desires for intimacy. However, emotional requirements can be more complicated. Many women seek out other women (girlfriends) for emotional support and friendship; sharing personal interests by getting involved in outside activities and group memberships.

Some women who have maintained this type of lifestyle, after many years, find it totally satisfying and doubt that they would give up their single status even if the right person should come along.

How does the professional male view the single career woman of today?

The generalized male viewpoint of today's single career woman is not altogether flattering and certainly not always accurate since it is often influenced by men with bruised egos.

The majority of men are frankly confused and threatened by ill- defined gender roles which have been altered significantly over the past 20 to 25 years. For example, the number of men who work full time has decreased over this period of time, while the number of women working full-time *and* part time has increased. The result of this change in status is that men are no longer seen as the sole financial provider for the family. Men see themselves as having lost their footing and are rapidly being reduced in professional as well as social prominence.

Basically, an unmarried, financially secure, independent female is 'a new breed of cat' to most men and they react in one of two ways:

They will try to push her down, figuratively, by accusing her of being too aggressive and hard-hitting, letting her know that she's too tough and that her defiance of tradition will render her incapable of succeeding in a man's world.

Another way some men react to a perceived threat to their masculinity is to go in the opposite direction by making an exaggerated effort to push the woman *up*. A good example of this phenomenon is the story of Claudia and her boss, Dan. From her first day on the job, Dan went out of his way to heap high praise on Claudia—lauding her courage, her energy and her intelligence; extolling her innumerable talents and accomplishments; defending her rights and arguing against any injustices that might threaten her.

At first, Claudia was thrilled. She felt she had found a real mentor, someone who would treat her as an equal. Six months later, Claudia was beginning to feel uneasy and troubled about her job, but she couldn't put her finger on anything specific. After eight months, Claudia *knew* that something was definitely wrong. Just before her year anniversary, Claudia abruptly resigned and went to work for a rival company—much to the shock and surprise of her co-workers.

What Claudia had wisely figured out was that Dan was anything but a mentor. Dan had cleverly placed her on a *pedestal* out of reach of the *important* decision making in the company. The way Dan boasted about her to clients and other members of executive level management, one would think that Claudia was right in the thick of everything. Instead, Claudia always found herself performing just on the fringe and never being allowed in the circle.

Obviously, Claudia couldn't take her problem to anyone in the company, because everyone considered Dan to be her champion. Who would believe her? There had been two other women in executive positions at the company who also left after brief tenures, but Claudia was told that their departures were due to "inadequate performances."

Men like Dan feel safe by placing a woman *up* on a pedestal—*outside* of what they perceive to be the *real* world where men are men and women are subservient.

Unfortunately, this is one of the times when a woman—because of her gender—does not have power. The only way she can escape from this pedestal is to *jump*—hopefully into another situation in which she can regain control.

When a woman does reach her goal in a career or profession, will she still have to battle male resistance?

Count on it.

Many career women who have spent years fighting their way into the male dominated professions must *continue* to wage battle, once inside, because vestiges of misogynist conduct *continue* to flourish.

A career woman taking her success for granted in a male dominated society is the same as leaving a virgin alone in a mountain cabin filled with men.

It's a matter of record that the general male population has long resisted the admittance of women into the upper levels of the business and professional worlds. Battles continue to be waged and camouflage continues to be engaged. It's apparent that women will feel this resistance for some generations to come.

Even though the majority of men pay verbal homage to the philosophy that women should be treated with respect and as equals, their actions belie their words and often support the *rumor* that sexist attitudes nevertheless exist. Even after a woman has become a doctor or lawyer, or has been elevated to corporate management, she will rarely be seen as *equal* in the eyes of her male colleagues. It's not that they don't recognize her achievements or understand that she's intelligent or gifted, it's just that most men feel compelled to take measures in defense of their power. (Translation: masculinity can be threatened by a self-sufficient woman.)

The woman, of course, will be outwardly approved by most of her male counterparts. A great deal of lip service will be paid to her as she is welcomed and invited to participate in the business at hand. What is unseen, however, are the invisible barricades that will prevent her from stepping over into sacred male territory.

A good example of this is the story of Carolyn, a young orthopedic surgeon who successfully completed her many years of training—"all without having to grow a penis" . . . she boasted to her friends.

After several years of private practice, Carolyn was asked to join a policy making committee at one of the hospitals where she operated. She readily accepted, hoping that she would get a chance to influence some changes she felt should be made. The committee consisted of eight people: seven male physicians and Carolyn.

At the first meeting, everyone made their introductions, then the chairman presented the committee agenda to be addressed by the members over the next year. During the next two meetings, Carolyn asked the chairman several questions. Each time, the chairman addressed Carolyn as "Karen"—despite the fact that she corrected him each time. For the third meeting, Carolyn decided to wear a wide sash across her chest -much like the type beauty queens wear—spelling out her name in large letters. Everyone laughed and thought it was a clever way to get her point across, except the chairman, who thereafter, avoided using her name at all.

In subsequent meetings, Carolyn frequently offered her views and suggestions on the issues being discussed. Remarkably, almost every time, the men *appeared* to listen, but as soon as Carolyn stopped talking, the men resumed their discussion as if Carolyn didn't exist and had never spoken. She felt pretty much like a clock ticking in an empty house.

To add insult to injury, one of the male physicians in the group would commonly bring up a point that Carolyn had made earlier in the meeting—as if it were *his* idea. The rest of the men, of course, would respond to him enthusiastically and Carolyn would get no credit.

Carolyn tried to express her frustrations to one of the male members who she thought would be most sympathetic. He did listen and he did agree with her, but nothing changed because he would not break rank and jeopardize his membership in the male "fraternity." Carolyn was obviously outnumbered and trying to fight the raging insecurities of seven threatened males would be like trying to put out a fire with doses of kerosene.

At the end of the year, Carolyn resigned her membership after deciding that any further attempt to shake the fragile foundation of male dominance would only engender more extreme defensive reactions. The animosity that would result certainly would not be worth it and her energies would obviously be better spent furthering her own practice.

As time went, by Carolyn would see these same committee members in the doctors' lounge or on the ward. She was friendly, of course, when she saw them and they would often chat casually about patients they had together or about hospital politics. Obviously, the mood of these one-on-one conversations was in sharp contrast to the cold indifference she had experienced during the committee meetings. It soon became apparent to Carolyn that her assertiveness in the meetings had presented a very blunt threat to the men and they had obviously raised their "shields" in unison to defend their masculinity. The only way that Carolyn could hope to ever make her views known at the hospital would be to encourage other women to join committees with her and eventually shift the balance of power.

Aren't some women just as guilty as men when it comes to chauvinism?

Definitely. Some women are guilty of conducting their working—and often social—relationships as if *all* men were enemies. This "chip-on-the-shoulder" and "I dare you to knock it off" attitude can only prove to be self defeating since a combative approach obviously destroys the very trust and loyalty that women seek.

It's important to remember that the roles of men—as well as women—are being redefined and in some ways, the transformation taking place may be more difficult for men. Women are adding dimension to their lives and gaining independence while men are being forced to shrink from what was once considered their major role—that of the provider for the dependent woman. Change is never easy—for anyone.

Obviously, the goal of every woman is to be judged on her *own* merit—not on her gender. A woman should certainly be able to apply that same fairness in judgment to a man.

What is the best way to handle sexism at work?

The *only* way is to consider the source. Most displays of sexism are a matter of perception since sexism is usually rooted in long-standing stereotypes and of course, stereotypes are like vampires—it takes centuries to get rid of them.

One example of a concept that is still with us: "It is proper for women to act one way and for men to act another way." For instance, a man and a woman pursuing a client might display a similar style of authoritative behavior. Someone else observing their efforts might *perceive* the woman's behavior negatively as "too aggressive" while the man's would be viewed positively as "appropriately assertive." Should the woman who is being viewed negatively take offense? Hardly. It would be about as pointless and inglorious as stepping in front of a bus.

In a business setting—when there is extreme frustration or anger—if a man reacts by swearing loudly, yelling, banging his fist on the table, etc. , his reaction will be seen as a sign of strength or forcefulness. If a woman reacts similarly, she probably will be considered "unstable." And, of course, the greatest "sin" of all for a woman to commit in a stressful

situation is to *cry* as a way to release her emotions. Undoubtedly, this will be viewed as the ultimate in weakness.

Has the focus on sexual harassment issues altered the workplace?

Most definitely. Some say the change has had a positive effect, while others complain it definitely has a downside.

In the "good old days," when a man touched a woman
inappropriately or told an off-color joke, the woman *slapped*
the man's face, which would serve to embarrass him—especially in front of others—and he would retreat. Today, an
offended woman *slaps* the man with a lawsuit.

There is something to be said for each of these tactics.
However, if a woman slaps a man today, she might get slapped
back!

The increased numbers of women in the workplace and
the subsequent conflicts that occur when males and females
work in close proximity has brought an awareness of sexual
harassment problems that previously were ignored. Today,
men and women both, are less afraid to confront the issues of
harassment and certainly less willing to remain quiet for fear
of losing their job.

Fear of lawsuits, hanging like threatening clouds, can
definitely change the climate of a working environment.
People are more cautious about what they say to someone of
the opposite sex, avoiding anything with sexual content, especially when it comes to humor. Physical contact is circum-
vented, friendships are limited and offers of assistance are
bypassed out of fear that they will be misinterpreted.

This anxiety and tension, of course, can have a negative
effect; causing confusion, limiting creativity and eliminating
certain aspects of the support systems that people count on
in the workplace.

We are definitely in a transitional stage with sexual harassment issues in the workplace. Sooner or later the pendu-

lum will drift back toward center, hopefully hovering somewhere between the slap in the face and the slap of a lawsuit.

Are women gaining numbers in male dominated fields?

Definitely. Some view the rate of increase with impatience, but undeniably, there is progress. Not only do women have more freedom to pursue their goals, but male business leaders are finding it politically as well as economically correct to move women into leadership positions.

Also, technological or scientific advances have encouraged women to enter fields usually restricted to men such as veterinary medicine, which used to require enormous physical strength for treating animals. Now, with the advent of powerful muscle relaxants and sophisticated anesthetics used in dart guns, etc., the issue of size and strength of a person in most cases is irrelevant.

Professional sports is another area where women are making tremendous inroads. Not only is there an increase in women's pro leagues, such as basketball and hockey, but publishers are producing sports magazines for women and marketers are fueling the growth and interest by providing young female consumers with sports-related items such as athletic shoes, helmets, etc. So the good news is: not only can a woman be successful in sports, she can sweat like a man and still be feminine.

The political arena has seen a sizable influx of women in recent years. And it really wasn't that long ago that the idea of women occupying the power seats of politics was an unlikely scenario since the image of a politician usually conjures up someone gritty, gutsy and hard—words that aren't commonly associated with the female gender.

Nevertheless, slowly but surely, as more and more women have entered the work force, become active in their communities and certainly taken more interest in their own voting participation, the images and views that shape the political climate has changed. The percentage of women entering politics has increased dramatically.

Are women gaining numbers in the corporate boardrooms?

It depends upon what statistical survey you read as to whether there is an increase or not. The consensus, however, is that in the general workplace, there is far more discrimination at the top of the ladder than there is at the bottom. There definitely is *some* increase over the past 20 years in the number of women listed as corporate board members but, once again, the consensus is that the growth is minimal.

This is obviously an area of emergence for women that will take some time, for several reasons: there are some men occupying key positions who *instinctively*—not always consciously—resent and therefore resist when it comes to allowing women to get ahead. Also, to reach this level of leadership, an individual must demonstrate a proven track record and, of course, women have only established themselves in the work force for a relatively short period of time, plus the doors to the corporate boardrooms have been open for even a shorter period of time.

Women are less likely to accept the long, strenuous work hours required to reach the boardroom and many prefer to give family obligations priority over work obligations.

Another factor that can prevent a *single* female from reaching the executive level is her marital status. Most male executives—especially in high-profile companies—have a wife who participates in the social requirements of his position. Often, these jobs are so demanding that it realistically takes two to do the job well. Therefore, a single woman has a handicap going in.

Any woman who has even come close to opening the doors of a corporate boardroom will admit that trying to pry open *any* traditional male environment takes some careful maneuvering—pretty much like trying to open an oyster with toothpick. It will take lots of time, lots of patience and most of all, an endless supply of prowess and pluck.

How should a woman dress in a professional environment?

Exactly as she pleases—within, of course, the parameters of appropriateness. What you wear reflects how you feel about yourself, whether you are a man *or* a woman.

Furthermore, you're a woman whether you hide behind a baggy floor-length smock or wear a fashionable, fitted dress. If you have a nice figure, there's nothing to be gained by hiding it.

Sexual differences cannot be totally put aside when men and women are working together. A man can work beside another man of a different color or race, but in time, the color or racial differences will be completely forgotten. However, a man working beside a women—no matter what her color or race—will *never* forget that she's a woman.

Charles Darwin once said, *"The very essence of an instinct is that it is followed independently of reason."*

CHAPTER SIX

"MARRIAGE IS LIKE LINGERIE—

IT ALL DEPENDS WHAT YOU PUT INTO IT'

*T*WO PEOPLE MEET *and fall in love. They feel that their greatest chance for happiness lies in their union and in their sharing what life will bring to them.*

As individuals, they view themselves as imperfect, but together they feel complete. Each satisfies the needs of the other and they decide to build a bridge that will connect their lives together.

But, a bridge cannot last forever.. it will need attention.

* * *

Is monogamy unnatural?

Simple logic dictates that it is.

If we as humans compare ourselves to animals—which is the closest we can get to a comparison by species—we see that most animals have an abbreviated level of sexuality (once or twice a year) compared to humans (once or twice a week).

So why do animals satisfy their limited urges with multiple mates while humans *try* to satisfy their limitless urges with just one mate?

Is monogamy an impediment to a healthy sex life?

Certainly not in the beginning. One of the more positive aspects of establishing a permanent sexual relationship with someone is that it brings relief to both partners. Since the pressure to search for suitable partners is gone, time and effort can be spent developing a mutual gratification by getting to know each other's sexual needs. Problems arise, however, when time passes and sexual desires become numbed.

For a woman—whose sexual drive is fed mostly through emotional input—a relationship that grows over the years can be increasingly satisfying. A man's sexual drive, however, being more compartmentalized and focused, requires additional innovative efforts as time goes by to relieve boredom and to prevent the sexual act from becoming a duty.

Once again, open and ongoing communication is the only foundation that can support lasting sexual compatibility.

Why get married at all?

If you're asking this question, you probably shouldn't.

It used to be the philosophy that marriage was the price men paid for sex—and sex was the price women paid for marriage. That, of course, has changed.

Also in the past, traditional marriage sprang from economic roots that were nurtured by strict sexual morality. The tradition was a simple one—not necessarily always a happy one. Women were expected to grow up, remain celibate, marry young and have children. Men were expected to grow up, find suitable employment, get married and support the family. Any man who put off marriage and avoided this responsibility was considered less than a man. And any woman who didn't marry was considered a spinster, or worse, if she pursued other interests.

Now, however—for both men and women—marriage is no longer a requirement, it's an option. The economic balance has shifted, ideology has dropped its facade and sex and sexuality are being served up a la carte rather than pre-fixed. Two people today—without the commitment of marriage— can live together, have children together and remain faithful to one another as long as they enjoy mutual gratification.

There are still those who prefer to stick with tradition and tie the knot that binds, but an overwhelming number of people are finding themselves comfortable with other options. As long as there is sexual and economic freedom— plus the added years to enjoy these freedoms—there will be those who choose to have multiple relationships.

Why do so many men resist marriage?

Generally, men feel an unconscious resistance to *returning* to a dependency on a female (their mother). Additionally, the idea of marriage has a way of stifling most men's sexual fantasies. The average man would love to pretend he was an endangered species and go through life having sex and impregnating as many women as possible.

Once men do surrender to marriage, however, they usually adjust rather quickly and discover marital bliss to be very gratifying. Ironically, for all of their resistance, men become far more emotionally dependent in a marriage than women do. Men need *anchoring*—someone to reassure them when they feel like failures or someone by their side to make them feel strong. It's a known fact that married men are happier, healthier and live longer than single men. Mortality studies have shown that marriage promotes survival for both men and women; however, single men seem to be more at risk than single women—probably because women, by nature, are the care givers and nurturers.

Women, of course, are usually eager to marry, but all too often their eagerness is inflated by idealistic expectations. Once the honeymoon is over and the day-to-day existence becomes reality, many women begin to realize that when they kissed the frog, hoping to turn him into Prince Charming, it might've been a better idea to forego the kiss and enjoy a delicious dinner of buttered frog legs instead.

What's the best way to overcome a man's resistance to marriage?

First of all, persistence—and equally important, patience.

It's never healthy for *anyone*—man or woman—to be co-erced into making a life-altering decision. And it's certainly never in a woman's best interest to push a man into marrying her. Even if she succeeds in getting him to agree, she won't really be happy knowing he accepted grudgingly.

It's always better to let time work its magic. Some people take longer to get used to an idea—needing more time to work through "hang-ups" so they can feel comfortable taking the step.

Of course, there is a fine line between how long is long enough to wait: usually until you feel like you've definitely run out of patience and you're tempted to tell him—"Okay, either fish or cut bait!"

Ultimatums, however, are risky at best. It would be wiser, instead, to wait for the proper moment to remind him that relationships—if they are to stay healthy—need to grow and move to the next level. The point should be made, calmly, that your relationship seems to have stagnated and therefore if it cannot move on to the next level—which is one of permanent commitment—that, perhaps, it would be best for both of you to start dating others.

Hopefully, this will serve as a "reality rubdown" for him and he'll wake up to the fact that he might just lose you to another man.

If the possibility of losing you doesn't pull his string, you are definitely better off letting the air out of that balloon. It's going nowhere.

Are pre-nuptial agreements a good idea?

Definitely. *Any* kind of marriage contract is better than none at all. Pre-nuptial agreements used to be a rarity but they are becoming increasingly more common.

Two people entering a business partnership usually draw up a legal agreement to protect their economic interests. Why shouldn't two people entering a long-term partnership as important as marriage protect their economic interests as well as those of their children to come?

Many people are put off by the idea because it isn't "romantic." Economic hardship, arguments over child custody and bitterness aren't romantic either, but they are often the realities of which divorce is made. Nobody likes to think about death, but most people draw up wills because they understand the fickleness of fate and how quickly life can change.

Ideally, marriage should last for life, but in the real world, eruptions do occur. It would seem wise, therefore, to enter into a pre-nuptial agreement when two people are in love and attitudes are positive.

Getting married without a contract is pretty much like dancing on a volcano. Things could stay calm . . . but you *never* know.

Should a woman keep her own name instead of taking her husband's name?

The answer to that question should be based on practicalities and circumstances that exist in the present as well as the future. Elimination of confusion should be the main concern—how a name change will affect a woman's professional status or how it will affect children.

A woman certainly is not going to be any more or less independent or self-confident one way or another.

Why do so many marriages fail?

Marriages today represent an even greater challenge than in the past when gender roles were clearly defined and people lived shorter lives. Today, men and women have been cast in new and confusing roles at home and at work. Now that women feel more "empowered," they often expect their mates to be adventuresome and strong, yet still be willing to share *equally* in the domestic chores. Many men can certainly relate to "adventuresome and strong"—after all, that's the way their fathers behaved. But they have far fewer points of reference when it comes to "domestic chores."

The need for compromise is greater now than ever before since couples find themselves struggling to establish their individual identities along with the other pressures that influence the equilibrium in a marriage. Also, in our present times, men and women can literally reinvent themselves at age 50 or 60 and start new lives. New beginnings often include shedding old habits—including mates.

Most people think that love, itself, will carry them through a marriage. The truth is that falling in love is easy. It just *happens* and you don't always know it's coming—sort of like an extra step at the bottom of the stairs. Marriage, on the other hand, is more like twirling a baton—it looks easy until you try it.

When people fall in love, the glow is intoxicating and they promise each other that their love will last forever. The truth, however, is that romantic love by its fragile, multi-faceted nature needs attention to survive. *It cannot be taken for granted*—especially in this day of sexual freedom, instant gratification and easy divorces.

What is the best way to satisfy a partner's needs?

The first step toward understanding a partner's needs is to take the time and effort to know what *your* needs are. A common complaint heard all too often in marriages is, "We are drifting apart, going in different directions." Usually, the fault lies in the fact that neither party has taken the time to analyze his or her own changing needs and therefore does not have a clue as to the other person's motivation.

It is difficult sometimes to understand what somebody else *really* needs because often what is verbalized is what is *wanted*—not needed—two very different things. It takes some effort, of course, but once you understand your own needs, you are more willing and able to understand and adjust to someone else's.

A good example is a woman who is shy and unsophisticated, marrying a worldly, high-profile man. At first, both of their needs are satisfied: hers, as an eager student and his as a patient instructor. As time passes, however, people evolve. The student may grow into an accomplished and cosmopolitan woman who wants a partner in her marriage rather than an instructor. If both parties understand their own changing needs and those of their partner's, they will be able to communicate their feelings and subsequently adjust, without feeling that they are being compromised.

Do women have to work harder than men to make a marriage work?

No question about it—but in defense of the male gender, they are not as *naturally* well equipped as women are to handle the emotional baggage that comes along with a marital trip.

It wasn't that long ago that subordination of the woman to the man was taken for granted in a marriage. Gender roles were very well defined. Now, of course, gender as well as marital roles have changed dramatically, requiring some experimentation—and most importantly, *negotiation*—to find the most comfortable way to structure the relationship.

Some characteristics, however, still remain a fact of life: Women by nature want to give as a gesture of their love. However, a woman should always remember that her desire to give will *not* be rewarded unless it is balanced by her ability *also* to withhold.

Married women like to discuss their lives with other women. Married men, on the other hand, prefer to use their leisure time pursuing hobbies *away* from the confines of the marriage.

Women not only handle emotion better than men, they often go looking for it in an effort to keep the lines of communication open. Most women agree that men just "don't listen." A wife's inclination is to probe every crevice of her husband's mind to search out his thoughts, his feelings, his doubts and his insecurities.

Men, of course, consider this kind of soul searching a threat and run from it like a turkey in November.

Can a woman give too much in a marriage?

As the marital relationship changes, some women become fearful that they might lose the love of their husband, and to combat this fear, they actually *give too much*—confusing giving with love. Women, by nature, are nurturers and givers—so it can be an easy trap to fall into.

It's important to remember that giving what is not wanted can be suffocating. A healthy relationship has to have a *balance* of give and take.

Change is inevitable in *every* relationship: marital, parent and child, siblings and even friends. Change is normal; not something to be feared. The ongoing challenge for a marriage is to first, recognize *when* a change occurs and secondly, *re-create* the environment that will allow love to remain. When the challenge is not met, love will eventually fade and be replaced by tolerance or guilt.

Is there anything wrong with someone marrying for money?

Only if you think there is.

There are as many *reasons* for marrying as there are people who make the decision. Whether the reasons prove to be "right" or "wrong" takes time—like waiting for a dish of yeast to proof.

Certainly, everyone views the world—and the part they play in the world—from different perspectives. Some people, with more materialistic views, see the world as a catalog of possessions. They review the inventory, then go about the business of getting their order filled.

Consider the story of twin sisters, Leslie and Laura. At the age of 20, Leslie decided to leave college and marry a very wealthy man who was ten years older than she. She confessed to Laura that she didn't actually love Donald, but that it would be okay because her needs were simple. "I only want the best," she laughed, " and Donald can make that happen.

Laura told Leslie that it was "wrong" to marry for money, that she should wait and marry for love. Leslie disagreed and married Donald a few months later.

Laura finished college and became a social worker. She

said that "helping people" was something she always wanted to do. Laura found a job counseling students at the local university and later fell in love and married James, who owned a small furniture store.

Leslie pursued hobbies, traveled with Donald and lived in a large home with a pool and tennis courts. Laura went to work in her husband's furniture store. She and James lived in a small home that they purchased inexpensively and fixed up.

Twenty years passed. Leslie's feelings for Donald had grown into love and their relationship was strong. Laura, on the other hand, began experiencing problems in her marriage with James once their children were grown. James and Laura eventually got a divorce and Laura went back to her job as a social worker.

Viewing these two marriages in hindsight, what appeared at the outset to be the *wrong* reason for Leslie and the *right* reason for Laura certainly changed with time. The moral of the story, of course, is that life is pretty unpredictable, like a mosquito in a nudist colony. You don't know who's going to get bit and where.

Do men really need a "boys' night out?"

Many men definitely do. They look forward to playing cards or drinking with no women around—being able to say and do whatever comes to mind, tell dirty jokes and just basically let their guard down.

Some women worry that a bunch of men getting together will be tempted to go looking for other women. This is generally not the case and certainly not the primary reason for "boys' night out" in the first place.

A lot of men say they enjoy the male "bonding" experience—getting together with other men to do "men things" such as roughing it in the woods for the weekend. By chopping wood, building fires and hunting for their own food, they basically attempt to reinforce their male sense of power and strength.

What is interesting is that when men get together for the purposes of male "bonding," there is far more a show of brute force than a show of words. Conversation is definitely kept to a minimum.

Women, on the other hand, who participate in a "girls' night out" or a woman's bonding experience, spend almost the entire time just talking and discussing emotional topics. Furthermore, a "girls' night out" usually occurs in the comfort of someone's livingroom.

Should a married couple spend periods of time away from each other?

It is usually healthier when this happens—the duration and frequency depends, of course, upon the two people involved.

Some couples can literally be together day and night and rarely need a *break*. Other couples hover on the brink of murder or mayhem if they're with each other more than two or three days a week. Even couples who fit together comfortably risk falling into one of the more common pitfalls in marriage—being taken for granted.

Sameness tends to dull the senses and distort reality, pretty much like watching an industrial training film over and over.

Does society treat men and women differently when it comes to infidelity during marriage?

Yes.

If a wife is unfaithful, the husband is usually viewed as "inadequate" and not man enough to satisfy the wife. On the other hand, society tends to have pity for a wife if her husband has an affair.

Women are notorious for "standing by her man" when he's been caught in the act. Some women will go so far as to be visibly supportive of the husband if his infidelity is publicized.

The reasons for these acts of female faith vary, of course, depending upon the individual and the circumstances. Some women handle this adversity through rationalization and denial because they refuse to admit that their husbands may have lost interest in them or don't love them anymore. Even though they may suspect their husbands of infidelity, they will make up "excuses" for them or push any suspicions totally out of their minds.

In some cases, money can be a factor. Divorcing a husband because he is unfaithful can jeopardize a woman's financial status. Some women put up with infidelity because they have a strong sense of commitment and feel they'd be deserting their man during a difficult time. They remain, and if anything—make an extra effort, believing that love alone will be strong enough to repair the rift.

Then, of course, there are women whose pride and self-esteem are so irreparably damaged by an unfaithful husband, they will seek a divorce no matter what the emotional or financial cost.

Whatever the reason for staying or leaving, adultery is bound to strike a blow in any marriage.

Is it normal for partners to distrust each other?

To some degree, yes.

Everyone comes equipped with a strong sense of self preservation. For instance, if you feel that you have given so much of your love to your partner—that you have basically surrendered yourself and placed your fate in your partner's hands—this realization can be a little unsettling at best. And if you feel that your partner has not given the same amount of love back to you, your reaction naturally would be one of distrust or hostility and your instinct would be to retreat.

In most cases, these lapses of trust are transient. An added show of love or a special gesture of affection usually offers the reassurances needed and returns the balance to normal.

Is jealousy a negative trait in a mate?

Jealousy, to some degree, is present in everyone and it's certainly one of the many ingredients that *should* be included in a relationship. The question is, of course, how much is healthy?

An absence of jealousy can be just as damaging as an oversupply. For instance, a husband who shows disinterest when another man propositions his wife is actually making a statement to his wife that says, "I don't really care about you." Indifference of this nature basically translates into rejection and a lack of love.

Constant displays of jealousy, on the other hand, will break down connections of trust and cripple a relationship. A fanatical desire to own somebody totally or possess someone with a selfish vigilance are traits born of extreme insecurity and fear. No love can exist in that type of environment.

Why do some women remain in a relationship where there is domestic violence?

Usually, abusive relationships start out in the same manner as other relationships—with both partners expressing love and tenderness toward the other. In time, however, love and tenderness are replaced by rage and violence.

Men that abuse women don't really consider them as partners in a relationship. They feel that women are supposed to "belong" to men, like property; that it is their right, along with their duty, to control women. They expect the woman to be subservient to them, to submit to all demands, including sexual and domestic. If the woman does not meet the man's expectations or worse yet, refuses his demands, he feels his power is being threatened and therefore, it is his "right" to exercise his control by use of violence.

The woman in this situation begins to think of herself as defective, because repeatedly, she has been told she is inadequate and inferior and has been beaten or abused because of it. The limited view she has of herself continues to narrow as more violence and abuse is heaped upon her. She lives her life in fear and, of course, the man encourages this fear because it's a power trip for him.

The woman feels she has no choice but to stay since there wouldn't be anybody who would want an "inferior" woman. All she can do is hope that in some way she can please this man who controls her. She fears that if she tries to escape, her rebellion will enrage him even more and he will hunt her down and destroy her.

Why do some people end up "henpecked" in a marriage?

Usually when this happens, a husband or wife is *allowing* it to happen.

The *henpeckee* is often without self respect and the *henpecker* feels only contempt. If the *henpeckee* stopped walking on eggs and stood up for his or her rights, the *henpecker* would probably scramble to attention and back down.

When henpecking becomes an established part of a marriage, the needs of *both* parties are obviously being satisfied.

How can a woman successfully make the switch from being "career tough" during the day to being soft at night for her mate?

By using one of her most valuable tools that a woman has: *flexibility.*

Once again, it's necessary to point out the realities of gender destiny. A man can be hard and aggressive at work *and* at play, he's expected to. A woman, on the other hand, can get away with being hard and aggressive at work, but not necessarily at play.

The transformation from tough to tender can be accomplished but it takes some valuable decompression time each evening to ease the transition; i.e., a drink and some music or a bath or shower and change of clothes.

Realistically, some schedules are so demanding that trying to arrange even a free five-minute period of time seems to be an impossibility. However, necessity is the mother of invention and relaxation and regeneration are certainly necessities when it comes to the health of a relationship.

What happens when a wife gains weight and a husband doesn't?

It depends upon how much importance was placed on looks and image in the first place.

A woman's metabolism changes with age, of course, but it is also altered dramatically after pregnancy, making weight control a definite challenge.

Unfortunately, some men—because of their own lack of confidence—feel personally diminished if their wives are no longer "fashionably thin." Even ten pounds can be viewed as a problem.

It's important to men like this that they be seen with women who are showpieces. They feel that anything less is an "insult" to their own self image. Obviously, a woman who gains even a relatively small amount of weight and is married to a man like this has a problem—and it's not the additional pounds. A husband this shallow, who measures life on such a superficial scale, is not about to change. Furthermore, as the wife gets older, a husband of this nature will only get more repulsed by her appearance and will most likely seek out younger, thinner women to support *his* image.

In addition, there are many men who feel very threatened by a *mature* looking woman (perhaps like their mother?) and feel more comfortable being around thin and frail women who appear to be vulnerable.

Obviously, there are men who do not fit either of the above descriptions, whose values allow them to reach deeper than superficial looks. A conflict about being fat, in this case, is engendered by the woman, herself, who is upset by her physical appearance.

Our present day culture pressures women to believe that the only way they can be beautiful is to be thin. Anything else is unacceptable. Therefore, some women who gain weight end up hating their bodies and feeling depressed when they cannot look the way that the movies and magazines say they should look. These feelings of inadequacy and self-loathing can obviously affect the marital relationship—even though the husband may be supportive. Hopefully, women can be realistic in their expectations and learn to accept their bodies despite of the dictates of the fashion world.

What happens when a husband gains weight?

Usually, very little—compared to when a wife puts on some pounds. Somehow, our popular culture is very accepting of "beefy" men—even encouraging it in some instances, such as the "fat cat" business executive who is displayed in the media as positive and powerful. A fat woman executive, on the other hand, would most likely arouse professional contempt rather than admiration.

In general, overweight men are described as "big" and overweight women are described as "fat" or "obese."

Men, generally, feel they are irresistible to women and are very proud of their bodies—no matter how they *really* look. Give a 300 pound man the opportunity to walk around naked and he'll do it in a flash without thinking twice. If you want further proof, go to the beach. It's common, unfortunately, to see men parading around with bulging bellies that look like huge hot air balloons anchored to tiny Speedo bathing suits the size of sling shots.

These are definitely not Kodak moments.

Why do some men show signs of jealousy when a baby arrives?

Men naturally respect, and in some cases, revere motherhood—because the concept of mothering brings to mind the gratification of all of *their* needs for nurturing and all of *their* desires for selfless devotion. So, when a husband sees his wife—the *current* woman in his life that nurtures him and devotes herself to him—giving all that "good stuff" to someone else, he might just get a little bent out of shape.

Some men literally revert to little boys when this happen; they feel neglected and in some cases, show outward signs of resentment toward the baby. The cure for this is to spread the attention around so that both father and baby feel like they're getting what they need. Of course, this does put an extra burden on the new mother, but in most cases, once the new father feels reassured, he grows up fast and assumes his new role.

Who should take care of the new baby—mother, father or other?

It would certainly make life easier for career parents if the roles of mother and father were interchangeable when it comes to child care. Unfortunately, in the working world, there is still a double standard: paternity leave is rare and stay-at-home dads are even more of an oddity. It is more *culturally* acceptable for the mother, rather than the father, to quit a job, or to take a leave of absence from a career in order to take care of a child or children at home. Additionally, many fathers involved in fast-paced, high-pressure jobs have little time to devote to family responsibilities since the workplace has made great strides toward assisting the working mother, but not the working father.

Even though motherhood (or fatherhood) is not as celebrated as career success, some parents prefer to stay at home based on their *own need* to spend as much time as possible with their children. Obviously, there are children with two working parents who grow up just as well as children with a stay-at-home parent.

One of the biggest considerations that influences the choices involved in child care is the financial structure of the family; whether both parents need to work, whether the household could get by with only one paycheck, or whether a "nanny" is a practical and acceptable option in the event that neither parent wants to stay home. Another important consideration, however, is the emotional one. If a woman, for instance, decides that financially she could afford to stay home, *should she?*

Some women who choose to stay at home at the expense of their careers, regret years later that they gave up their opportunity for power or fame or financial rewards. Also, women who do not build a career for themselves feel vulnerable if the marriage ends in divorce, or if a husband becomes ill or disabled.

Other women who return to work and never quite achieve the successes they had hoped for, sometimes look back and think they could have just as well spent that time at home with their child.

Choosing between career parenting and staying at home can be a difficult decision to make; and when asked if it was the right choice, it's the kind of decision that won't produce a "right or wrong" answer until much later in life.

Is it really possible for a woman to successfully manage a career and a family?

Of course, but it's imperative to keep expectations *realistic* and to keep in mind the old saying: "A woman's work is never done . . . *by a man."*

Above all, a career woman needs help—however, most of that help will no doubt have to come from the "outside." If the husband is involved in his own career, he probably won't be able to offer adequate assistance.

Generally, men today do more housekeeping chores than their fathers or grandfathers ever did or even thought of doing. In those "good old days," the wife had a delicious, carefully prepared meal on the table when the husband came home from work; she met him at the door, wearing a pretty dress and a ribbon in her hair; and the children were carefully scrubbed and clean. Today, when the husband comes home from work, chances are he's greeted by a message on the answering machine telling him the wife will be late, because she's stopping at the cosmetic counter at the department store for a makeover and that he can take some frozen dinners out of the freezer and put them in the microwave after he drives the baby sitter home.

The modern man of today, who will don an apron and consent to separating whites from colors in the laundry, has "surrendered" his long-standing privileged stance—contrary to his wishes—and will, in most cases, silently resent his new role.

Most of the time, the responsibility of the home is still being carried primarily by women. If given any choice in the selection of household duties, men will gravitate toward outside chores like lawn maintenance or house repairs. Inside chores like cooking, laundry, cleaning, and grocery shopping—which are far more constant and time consuming—usually fall to the woman. Even if a man *offers* to clean the house, chances are, the woman won't be satisfied. A man's concept of "clean" in most cases comes nowhere near a woman's concept—like comparing the Little League to the Major League.

Most husbands share the load when it comes to logistical needs, such as car pools and doctor appointments. However, for emotional support, such as problems at school or with friends, or for social support such as decisions on outside activities, etc., children most often turn to their mothers.

There are only so many hours in so many days to accomplish first of all, what a woman *needs* to do and then, what she *wants* to do. She can't expect to turn in a quality performance at her office, be present at a child's activities, meet her husband for an afternoon's rendezvous and still squeeze in a French lesson so she'll be prepared for her trip to Paris next month.

There are way too many options in our lives to choose from—anywhere from flavors of coffee to television channels to models of automobiles. Just the decisions themselves take time and energy—the two things in our lives that we have in limited supplies.

All of us want it *all*—but the smart ones figure out that all is *never enough* and that it's human nature to want more.

Has the definition of motherhood changed now that women's roles have changed?

Not really. Schedules may be tighter and activities may be different, but when a woman is a mother, her instincts toward her children are the same whether she calls herself a homemaker or an astronaut.

A modern mother today—like a mother hundreds of years ago—will spend her life trying to save her children from making mistakes. And like all the mothers before her, she will agonize over the balance of giving enough or too much to her children.

Raising a child has always been and still is like reading a long mystery—you have to wait for a generation to see how it turns out.

Should a woman ask a man to have a vasectomy versus tying her tubes?

In the past, sterilization was a subject that men completely avoided. Today, however, men are being asked to take a shared responsibility. This should be a decision that *both* parties weigh in on equally.

Obviously, men are going to be resistant and even squeamish when it comes to the question of someone "tinkering" with their manhood, even though a vasectomy has proven to be a safe and relatively minor procedure. Tying a woman's tubes, on the other hand, is more invasive.

Many women, unfortunately, "give in" and let their husbands off the hook, rationalizing that they should be the one to take the action because they are more used to pain and medical intervention than men are.

This, of course, is not the *healthiest*—and certainly not the most fair—way to make this decision. Both parties should consult with their physicians and become as knowledgeable as possible about both sterilization methods. The physical and mental conditions of *both* parties should be the primary concerns.

Who suffers more psychological damage in a divorce—men or women?

It all depends upon the self esteem of the individuals involved. Of course, it also depends upon the financial security that each is left with.

If both the husband and wife are working in independent careers where each has established an active, professional life outside the marriage, their separation—albeit difficult—would not throw either of them into a serious state of desperation due to loss of income, lack of purpose or a feeling of uselessness.

On the other hand, if a husband who is powerful and highly visible divorces his wife—who has not established any real identity outside of being "the wife"—she will have an extremely difficult time adjusting to the divorce. Not only will she be losing a mate, she will undoubtedly lose the majority, if not all, of the friends that went along with the marriage—because, obviously, she will not be able to offer these "friends" as much as her high-profile husband can.

The lesson to be learned, of course, is to establish your own identity and *not* be dependent upon someone else's.

Whatever happened to the prince and princess who married and lived happily ever after?

They are still with us—in children's dreams and maybe a few adults who still have such fantasies.

Everyone, unconsciously, wants to believe in fairy tales. That is why people live vicariously through celebrities who *appear* to be living the real life fairy tale. Of course, these people are then devastated when tragedy befalls that celebrity or they feel betrayed when the celebrity's actions prove to be less than what is expected. Fairy tales have always been a part of women's lives—much more so than men's—because women have always been sheltered and partitioned away from the real world, whereas men were encouraged to go out and actively seek adventure. Women, therefore, could only pursue their fantasies through fairy tales while men pursued theirs in the in the real world.

Now, of course, childhood fairy tales become only snapshots from the past for many women since they too can go out of the home and seek adventure in the real world. Deep down, however, we all have some fairy tales that we dream will come true and sometimes they do—even though it may take a little re-writing in our minds.

CHAPTER SEVEN

"WHEN MENOPAUSE APPEARS—

YOU CAN'T PUT A GENIE BACK IN A LAMP"

*I*T HAS ARRIVED . . . *summoned by the passage of time. It may not be what you'd wish for, but menopause will certainly change your life.*

No matter in what century a woman lives, no matter what her station or occupation in life; she is defined by the three stages of her biological inheritance: youth and virginity, womanhood and the ability to bear a child, then menopause and infertility.

This pre-destined rhythm of the female is a certainty that can be accepted; it can be viewed as a handicap; or it can be suppressed and disguised—but in no way can menopause be ignored.

* * *

Why do so many women fear menopause?

Menopause has long been a taboo subject, because it's onset had always heralded old age and the end of life. A woman who was approaching the "menopausal age," used to feel like the proverbial bug, waiting for the windshield of life to "hit" her.

Of course, those were the days when women lived only until their fifties or early sixties. Today, that is no longer true. The life expectancy of women today extends well into the 80's, which means that a woman who has reached menopause has approximately 30-plus years ahead of her—a third of her entire lifetime.

Women experience menopause anywhere from 45 to 55—with an average age of about 50. The onset of menopause (perimenopause) is usually determined by hereditary factors as well as general physical condition.

In the past, the subject of menopause was never discussed openly, but was relegated to secret talks between women. It was also a subject that physicians preferred to avoid, treating only the physical symptoms that women presented during menopause.

Today, unfortunately, many physicians still fail to take the time to educate women on the subject of menopause. However, the good news is that now, there are endless sources of information about menopause openly available from libraries, bookstores, magazines and the Internet.

Menopause hasn't changed, but it's significance has.

There are so many wild stories about menopause—what actually happens?

There is really no mystery to the menopause process—it is simply the reverse of the menstruation process.

Several years before the first menstrual period, the ovaries in a young girl's body gradually begin to produce the female sex hormones, estrogen and progesterone. During the reproductive years, the ovaries release an egg each month and at that time, the level of sex hormones increases for the purpose of thickening the lining of the uterus. This step is in preparation for the fertilization of the egg. If fertilization does not occur, the level of sex hormones decreases and the lining of the uterus sloughs off; this is the menstrual period.

The cycle repeats itself monthly for approximately the next 30 to 40 years, at which time the onset of menopause begins: the ovaries eventually stop releasing eggs, the production of estrogen and progesterone declines and the lining of the uterus no longer sloughs off. When menstrual periods have stopped for a year, the menopause is considered complete. Obviously, this is a gradual process, in the same way that the process preceding menstruation does not happen overnight.

Just as the young girl, entering the menstrual phase of her life, experiences signs and symptoms as her sexual hormone levels *rise*, a woman entering the menopausal phase of her life experiences signs and symptoms as her sexual hormone levels *fall*.

Why do so many women approaching 40 complain that they're "running out of eggs?"

Unless they're talking about the supply in their refrigerator—women in this age range *are* running out of eggs in their ovaries.

At birth, a woman's ovaries hold all the eggs she will *ever* have—well over 100,000. These eggs are not "fresh"—they're "hibernating," carefully wrapped up in tiny sacs, or follicles. When a girl reaches the age of 10 to 13, ovulation begins; her ovaries produce estrogen and the cycles start. Each month, several follicles ripen; but usually just one egg—the first to mature—is released from an ovary. The other few eggs that didn't develop as fast, just stop growing.

This "production line" is repeated every month—winter, summer, rain or shine. Normally, about age 40, a woman will have only about 5,000 to 10,000 eggs left. Of course, the countdown continues as each month passes. When the ovaries finally run out of eggs, the estrogen supply runs out also. Women will experience an early menopause if they are born with fewer eggs than average or if their ovaries release more than the usual amount of eggs during a cycle.

What are the most common 'first signs' of menopause?

Menopause is highly individualized. Just as menstrual periods differ for each woman, so does menopause. Some women sail through the menopause with minimal physical or mental discomfort. Others experience radical changes and upheaval in their lives.

Two of the most common signs of menopause are irregular periods and hot flashes. When periods become irregular, they can be longer or shorter than usual and often the bleeding is heavier than usual. Sometimes, there can be bleeding between the periods.

Usually one of the first signs of menopause, is hot flashes—a direct result of the lower level of sexual hormones in the body. When this happens, the skin on a woman's face and chest will "blush"; she will feel hot and perspire. Hot flashes usually last a few minutes but can occur anytime day or night. Depending upon the woman, hot flashes usually last anywhere from one to two years. The most common relief for hot flashes is hormone therapy—a treatment that attempts to replenish the body's depleting hormone supply.

Why is there so much controversy about hormone replacement therapy?

Because there have been so many studies done—with conflicting results. Some have shown that estrogen can increase the risk of breast cancer, while others have shown there is very little risk. Apparently, there is no definitive yes or no answer to the question. Many women, of course, find this lack of a "clear answer" worrisome. However, worry is like a rocking chair .. it gives you something to do, but it doesn't get you anywhere. The best course of action for every woman is to do her own "research" and learn the facts for herself.

There are two kinds of hormone therapy: estrogen for women who have had their uterus removed and estrogen combined with progesterone for women who still have their uterus. Progesterone has been proven to help prevent cancer of the uterus.

There have been conclusive studies done that show a direct correlation between estrogen deficiency and porous bones or "osteoporosis"—loss of bone tissue resulting in bones becoming thin and brittle. This, of course, can lead to bone fractures—very often, hip fractures or vertebral fractures which results in curvature of the spine. There is no treatment available to repair or replenish the loss of bone tissue. Once estrogen levels begin to fall, bone loss begins to occur. Estrogen therapy started *after* estrogen levels have dropped will stop further progression of bone loss, but it will not replenish the bone tissue already lost.

Some studies have also shown that estrogen can prevent heart attacks and strokes in woman after menopause. If a woman has a family history of cardiovascular disease or other risk factors such as smoking, obesity or high blood pressure, hormone therapy should certainly be a consideration.

In pre-menopausal women, where hormone levels fluctuate more dramatically and unpredictably, finding the right hormone treatment can often be a matter of trial and error. In post-menopausal women, there appears to be less of a challenge, once the hormone levels have stabilized.

Obviously, there are benefits to hormone therapy but there also can be risks. Health decisions are never easy, especially when there are so many facts, figures and claims to wade through. The good news, however, is that there *are* options. It wasn't that long ago that women had to endure the symptoms and the unfortunate aftermath of menopause without *any* help.

In the final analysis, each woman has to make her own *informed* decision. This is accomplished by first, educating herself as to the various forms of hormone therapies that are available; consulting with an experienced physician; and finally, evaluating her family history and the condition of her health at the time of menopause.

What are the emotional problems a woman can experience during menopause?

Many women complain of mood swings, insomnia, depression or anxiety. It's true that hormone levels affect many areas of the body, including the digestive tract, bones, breasts, urinary tract, etc. Altered hormone levels also affect the body's endocrine system which controls metabolism and of course, metabolism influences a person's weight.

There are conflicting medical findings as to whether the fluctuating hormone levels experienced during menopause are the cause of psychological problems or does the problem lie with other mid-life crises and changes that can occur in a woman's life at the time of menopause. The impending loss of reproductive ability is usually far outweighed by a "domestic" crisis, such as children leaving home, aging parents, retirement, financial stresses, divorce or widowhood. These problems become much more difficult to handle when they are complicated by hormonal instability and fears of becoming less physically desirable.

The women who seem to experience the most stress are those who traditionally have neglected any personal pursuits earlier in life, having devoted their adult lives to raising children and seeing to the needs of the family. When the children are grown and gone and the husband is at the peak of his career, these women are suddenly left without a purpose: the once-needed mother and homemaker is alone with a lifetime to fill. Menopause becomes a symbolic confirmation that they are entering the "older woman" stage of life.

Other women, however, who have had more dimension in their lives realize that menopause can actually be the *beginning* of the best time in their lives.

Logically, in many cases, it is difficult to separate the physical from the mental. However, whatever the reason, if a woman is experiencing emotional problems during menopause, it's important to get help and support from a physician and/or therapist; and sometimes, just using a very close friend as a sounding board can help a woman to sort out what's going on her life and where the stresses are.

What effect does menopause have on sexual activity?

The only *direct* effect of reduced hormone levels on sexual activity appears to be a physical change in delicate tissues. The lining of the vagina becomes thinner and drier due to less secretion; this can result in tenderness, inflammation ands sometimes, painful intercourse. However, estrogen replacement therapy and estrogen creams applied directly to the tissues usually correct any problems.

Occasionally, women will express a general disinterest in sexual activity during menopause, but the reasons for this disinterest usually point to factors other than hormonal changes; i.e., psychological problems, difficulty with interpersonal relationships, or side effects of medications they may be taking at the time.

Some women fear menopause, thinking that they will no longer be desirable and will lose their sexuality. Of course, sexuality is a matter of attitude and the best way to combat this fear is to eliminate the mystery by understanding the dynamics of menopause.

A great many women actually experience an increase in sexual activity after menopause—almost a feeling of *freedom*. The risk of getting pregnant is a thing of the past, they no longer have the problems and inconvenience of menstrual periods and best of all, they have earned the feeling of self confidence than only years of experience and insight can bring. Some women claim that it was only after menopause, that they really started to enjoy sex.

What is surgical menopause?

Prior to menopause, if a woman has her ovaries removed, the estrogen supply once produced by the ovaries will abruptly cease. If there is no hormone therapy to replace the lost estrogen, symptoms of menopause, such as hot flashes, will occur—most likely in an abrupt manner. If only one ovary is removed, the other ovary will continue producing hormones.

If a pre-menopausal woman has only her uterus removed (hysterectomy) and the ovaries remain, she will not have symptoms of menopause until the ovaries decline in function normally.

How can a woman prepare for menopause?

The same way a porcupine prepares for cold weather: eat well and stay sharp. You'll be able to handle whatever "perils" the changing environment sends your way.

Good nutrition is important throughout *all* of a woman's

life, but especially during the years of menopause. Foods high in calcium are very important as an aid in the prevention and treatment of bone loss. Foods low in fat, along with fruits, vegetables and whole grain products all contribute to a healthy and well functioning body.

Exercise is particularly essential as a woman gets older. Regular exercise not only regulates weight, it helps the heart, improves mental health and builds bone mass.

Establishing healthy eating and exercise habits *early* in life will provide a "comfortable cushion" for a woman to fall back on—instead of trying to establish new habits in the middle of a transition.

Above all, attitude and knowledge—plus a sense of humor—are the main determinants when it comes to negotiating a smooth transition. The more a woman knows about menopause, the better her ability to handle the challenges. Menopause is not a fixed condition; even though your ovaries are treating your body temperature like a yo-yo, you can be reassured it's going to pass.

A great deal has been written about female menopause. Don't men go through a similar change?

Yes. Men can experience a form of male menopause—usually occurring somewhere between ages 40 to 70. In Europe, this is referred to as "Viropause" or "Andropause."

Male menopause is a result of decreased hormonal activity as well as the general aging process. Men *do not* become infertile as women do during menopause. Men may experience occasional failure in maintaining an erection and this, of course, can be very frightening, especially to a man who has taken his "virility" for granted.

Some men go to their doctor for hormonal replacement shots or medicinal aids to enhance erection. Other men chase young women to reaffirm their youth or seek out cosmetic surgery to reassure themselves. Still others panic and experience periods of impotency, fearing that a decline in sexual potency means a plunge to ground zero. Of course, it doesn't. Male menopause should only be a transitional period.

The wife or lover of a man going through male menopause can often find herself in the role of an injured bystander when the man reacts to these changes by retreating. When this happens, the mate or lover may feel that the man's sexual indifference is her fault, that perhaps she has become less attractive or is no longer desirable to him.

Once again, open lines of communication are crucial to surmounting the problem.

Is male menopause considered as difficult for men as it is for women?

Let's just say that, from the looks of it, male menopause is more fun. Women get treated with hormones while men treat themselves to younger women and fast cars. And, let's face it, if men suffered from hot flashes, menopause would be declared a reason for promotion to a corner office where there was better circulation and cooler temperatures.

Men who were relentless in their sexual appetites and dependent upon sexual prowess as the mainstay of their lives, will obviously have a tougher time dealing with a downward shift in virility than men whose sexual appetites were more in balance with the rest of their lives.

Generally speaking, male menopause can be far more alarming for a man because it threatens the very core of his manhood: his sexuality. Female menopause, albeit significant, marks the end of a woman's fertility, but does not impinge upon her sexuality.

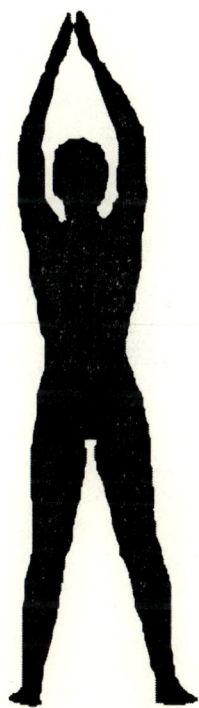

CHAPTER EIGHT

"AGING—START YOUNG

TO GUARANTEE SUCCESS"

*L*IFE IS LIKE *love. You start out with exuberance and idealism and even as the years go by and you mellow, you deny the fact that it will ever end.*

* * *

What are the secrets to maturing gracefully?

The first secret is *preparation*.

The beauty that a young woman has comes naturally; it's given to her. Mature beauty, however, reflects what a woman *has done* over the years to enhance the natural beauty she was born with.

When you're young and you look in the mirror, it's almost impossible to imagine that the reflection you see will change. You have visual proof in front of you, confirming that you have a firm body and a youthful face. Even when you indulge in excesses or give in to temptation or neglect, your reflection is there to reassure you that, sure enough, nothing *appears* to be affected.

The truth, however, is that time moves faster than a pickpocket; before you know it, the years are gone. The pleasing reflection you *used to see* has evaporated before your eyes like a soap bubble.

Good genes can certainly contribute to how well one ages, but obviously, inheritance can't swim against the tide of time without some help. Careless eating and exercise habits and poor skin care will inevitably take their toll to the point where even plastic surgery cannot recoup the losses.

The second secret to maturing gracefully is *awareness,* born of a hard-won self esteem. A woman will make sacrifices and compromises and she will most likely experience sorrow during her lifetime. As she gets older, a woman may look back and think to herself with some regret that perhaps she didn't do all the things she could have done, or even should have done. Few people do.

Despite all the material gains and losses that are accumulated in a lifetime, the reality remains that in the final analysis, everything we have is borrowed. The *only* things we ever truly own are the knowledge we have collected and the confidence we have gained in ourselves.

After our lives have eaten up the years and the only thing left is food for thought, it is easy to see who is content and who is bitter and unfulfilled. How people feel about themselves certainly affects everyone around them.

When an older man shows contentment, it will be because he has achieved his peace of mind through acceptance. (You fight it when you're young and you accept it when you're older.) He will smile easily and his mood will be mellow.

When an older woman shows contentment, it will be because she has achieved her peace of mind by first, *understanding* herself and then, by accepting. An older woman, will also smile easily and her mood will be mellow, but in addition—because she is richer due to her *awareness*—she will also have a certain *radiance* that is unmistakable.

Should an older person take advantage of the advances in cosmetic surgery?

If a person wants to look "better"—it's a good idea. "Looking better" *used* to be the aim of cosmetic surgery. Now, however, the big push is to make people look "younger." People in their 20's, 30's and 40's are flocking to the plastic surgeons for liposuction, tummy tucks and buttock lifts. In our society—now more than ever before—"old" definitely means useless and defective. People are actually frightened to show any sign of age. The prevalent attitude is: if you're over 50 and show it at all, forget it—you might as well park yourself on a block of ice in the middle of the ocean—you're history.

Desperate attempts at anti-aging, of course, are futile. If a 60 year-old woman wants to look better by getting an eye lift, why not? But there's no way that the same 60 year-old woman can look 30 again. And why should she?

How does the aging process differ for men and women?

In the beginning of a relationship, both men and women desire to impress and so they take the time and effort to dress fashionably and maintain good grooming. Once the relationship gets comfortable, however, most men seem to place fashion and grooming in the category of "special occasion." Women, on the other hand, seem to devote more of their energies to fashion and grooming in an effort to keep the fantasy alive as long as possible.

In a youth oriented society, men are admired as they age and women are pretty much discarded and/or disregarded as they age. The physical looks of older men are considered to be distinguished or sophisticated, however, an older woman is just *that*—an "older woman."

From a psychological standpoint, aging can be frightening for a man because of his gradual loss of virility. For a woman, it can be traumatic because of her gradual loss of physical looks.

Sexually, a man's capacity declines with age sometimes to the point of impotency. A woman, on the other hand, can maintain her sexual capacity well into her 80's depending upon her physical health. This *inequity* in an older couple often reinforces a man's resentment of a woman's power over sex.

Doesn't aging bring on weight gain no matter what you do?

To some extent, yes. From a physiological standpoint, metabolism shifts as time passes and the level of activity diminishes. Logically, food intake should be appropriately reduced to fall in line with these changes and that's where the greatest challenge lies.

There's also, of course, the emotional component which is the predominant factor in weight control. When a woman ages, the negative realities of her life can pressure her into very destructive eating habits.

For example, Margaret, in her late 40's, felt that her marriage and her life in general had not lived up to her expectations. In the past, she had always maintained a slim body and was conscientious about her health habits. Now, with her children grown, her career stagnating and her husband, pretty much indifferent to her, she felt angry and frustrated and turned to food for comfort.

Eating became a form of companionship for her. She constantly felt hungry—but in reality, this was not a hunger of her body but of her mind. As her husband increasingly withdrew from her sexually, she turned to food again, seeking sensual pleasure.

As her body increased in size, her self-loathing increased and she sank into depression. The thought of trying to take control of her life seemed far more threatening than the path of self destruction she was already on.

Fortunately, Margaret's sister intervened and persuaded Margaret to get professional help before it was too late. Both Margaret and her husband did go into therapy, and hopefully, will be able to turn their lives around.

Why are women so much more obsessed with weight gain than men?

Because we all want to live up to ideals—to be loved, admired, and accepted—and in our modern society, the "ideal" woman has the body of a lean adolescent girl, whereas society's "ideal" man has a developed, muscular body.

It becomes immediately apparent to anyone analyzing these "standards" that for men, the pursuit of attaining his ideal is a healthy one and for women, the pursuit in most cases is downright *unhealthy*. Nevertheless, the ideals of fashion continue to dictate.

A relatively short time ago—in the early 1900's—the "ideal" woman was somewhat obese. Furthermore, a woman in those days who was naturally thin was encouraged to eat more to put on some fat! Since history does indeed repeat itself, there is hope that in time to come, the "Reubenesque" woman will be held up as the ideal. Once again, timing is everything.

The reality—in any era—is that real beauty never fits any one particular mold. However, knowing that to be true and being comfortable with it can be two different things. A person's self image is pivotal to life and everything else revolves around it.

Can an older couple still enjoy sex when there are physical limitations?

Of course. Sexual pleasure and satisfaction comes in many forms—like cuddling and fondling—not just through intercourse.

Understanding each other's needs is the main requirement at any age. However, a good dose of patience and a sense of humor can go a long way towards maintaining sexual happiness as the years go by.

A good example of this is the famous story of "Gertie" and "Sid"—both in their eighties. One night, Gertie called downstairs to Sid, asking him to come upstairs and make love to her. Sid replied that he could only do "one or the other!" Hopefully, Gertie opted to go downstairs and join Sid on the couch.

Will the new anti-impotence drugs for men change the sex lives of older people?

Without a doubt.

The drug, Viagra, was developed to help men who are impotent, who cannot sustain an erection. However, apparently the opportunity for "increased virility" is too good to pass up for any man—not necessarily impotent—who feels that his performance could be enhanced by the drug. Sales of Viagra has skyrocketed as men are running—not walking—to their urologists to get the pill that will make them more virile.

The basic theory behind the drug is amazingly simple: when you relax the muscles in the penis, more blood will be allowed to flow in and thereby sustain an erection. The drug works in a large number of cases—with reportedly minimal physical side effects—and has definitely made an improvement in people's lives. Many women—as well as men—are delighted that the availability of Viagra will enable them to have a more active sex life with their mates.

On the other hand, it can also cause some problems in people's lives. Some women, after 30 plus years of marriage, for example, consider sex to be a slightly silly indulgence and have settled into a "comfortable" routine with their mates. When they were younger, they probably had sex six nights a week. Now, they have sex, on the average, maybe once or twice a month.

With the advent of Viagra, all a man has to do is pop the pill and in an hour, he's like a gorilla in heat. But wait a minute—the woman is about the same age as the man; they both have slowed down to some extent and certainly tire a lot easier than they used to. Sex does take energy. If the man has gotten his battery charged with an aphrodisiac and the woman hasn't, what happens then? In many cases, nothing.

Some women fear that if they aren't interested in stepping up the pace of their sexual life, that the men will pack up their little blue pills and go elsewhere.

Obviously, the anti-impotence drugs are going to change people's sexual expectations and in the majority of cases, that's going to be a beneficial change. Often, just the power of suggestion can have a positive effect: In Italy, someone has come out with *"Viagra gelato,"* available in blue or pink "flavors." There is no Viagra in it, of course, but still, the sales have proven to be extraordinary and the demand increases daily.

How can a couple avoid conflict when they both retire and find themselves at home together all the time?

So much depends upon the individuals involved. Some couples don't miss a beat when retirement comes. They effortlessly slip into a schedule of doing everything together, including hobbies as well as dining together.

Other couples know, from past experiences, that "togetherness" is a sure formula for a murder-suicide, so they make a concerted effort to plan their separate schedules and go their own ways the majority of the time.

Still other couples find it best to compromise. They choose activities that they both like doing together and the rest of the time, pursue their own individual interests.

Some women who have not worked and used the home as a base for various activities, might resent suddenly having a man under foot every day while trying to conduct normal activities. Obviously, the man's daily routine has changed and in this situation, the woman will be forced to make adjustments in her routine as well, so that both of them can occupy the same "space" and still maintain their own identities.

Avoiding conflict at the time of retirement often takes some time, but it is definitely worth the effort.

Why do some older woman adjust to losing a longtime mate easier than others?

It depends upon the extent of their personal "investment."

The best way to soften the blow of losing a mate is by *preventative* measures: establishing your own life in addition to your life with your mate.

For example, carrying two baskets of eggs is better than

carrying one—because you are better balanced and if you should lose one, you'll always have the other.

Losing someone through divorce or death can be very painful. It used to be that "grieving" was reserved for widows only. Nowadays, however, as life spans reach well into the 80's and 90's, couples are getting divorced after 30, 40 and even 50 years of marriage. When you are an older woman, suddenly alone, you feel the loss no matter what the cause.

How much loss you feel is directly related to how much of yourself you put into the marriage—all the bits and blocks of emotion and feelings that you gave to your partner. You are, realistically, losing that part of yourself.

Ironically, this is one time when shallow women fare better, because they have given so much less. However, shallow women are never able to extract the real joys and rewards from life.

Why is there such a stigma to being old?

There is an *old* saying that age is only a state of mind—provided you have one left! Our society as a rule, however, often considers old age to be an incurable illness.

Instead of admiring an older person's wisdom and achievements, those who are younger all too often regard an aging person as defective. Youth and vigor are held up as the norm while aging is viewed as a dreaded malady burdened with griefs and infirmities.

This is actually a loss for all concerned. A young woman, for example, could benefit greatly from an older woman's knowledge and experience. Human beings are prepared from the moment of their birth to extract the best out of life until the time when they will eventually *leave* life. Animals, on the other hand, are prepared from the moment of birth to spend their lives defending against the probability that they will suddenly *lose* life.

In some societies old people are loved and respected for their contributions. Furthermore, these old people are allowed to *leave* life when their time comes *naturally*. And because they are loved, they can die with calm and contentment.

When people's lives are prolonged through the bravado of scientific achievements, there is no dignity. And when people are cared for only out of duty and then die in the absence of love, their death is sadly without serenity.

Because of the pervasiveness of a negative attitude of the aged, those who are old feel shunned and even though they may not be ill, they are made to feel that they are dying— *without* the peace that death itself brings.

Can a woman who has reached the "winter" of her life still enjoy being a woman?

As a female, you are not born a woman. You *become* a woman. And once this goal is achieved you are a woman for *all* seasons.

* * *

There are few mysteries left to explore in our media savvy world of today. The only real secrets worth pursuing are those we find along the trail leading to ourselves.

When a woman discovers the potential of her femininity, she discovers the incredible power she holds within her feminine grasp.

Knowledge leads to power . . . power gives pleasure . . . and pleasure is getting what you want.

It's exciting to be a woman.

Enjoy.

* * *

-NEIM